T0286808

Cambridge Elements ☰

Elements in the Philosophy of Ludwig Wittgenstein
edited by
David G. Stern
University of Iowa

WITTGENSTEIN ON FORMS OF LIFE

Anna Boncompagni
University of California, Irvine

CAMBRIDGE
UNIVERSITY PRESS

Shaftesbury Road, Cambridge CB2 8EA, United Kingdom

One Liberty Plaza, 20th Floor, New York, NY 10006, USA

477 Williamstown Road, Port Melbourne, VIC 3207, Australia

314–321, 3rd Floor, Plot 3, Splendor Forum, Jasola District Centre, New Delhi – 110025, India

103 Penang Road, #05-06/07, Visioncrest Commercial, Singapore 238467

Cambridge University Press is part of Cambridge University Press & Assessment, a department of the University of Cambridge.

We share the University's mission to contribute to society through the pursuit of education, learning and research at the highest international levels of excellence.

www.cambridge.org
Information on this title: www.cambridge.org/9781108931151

DOI: 10.1017/9781108946513

First published 2022

A catalogue record for this publication is available from the British Library.

ISBN 978-1-108-93115-1 Paperback
ISSN 2632-7112 (online)
ISSN 2632-7104 (print)

Wittgenstein on Forms of Life

Elements in the Philosophy of Ludwig Wittgenstein

DOI: 10.1017/9781108946513
First published online: September 2022

Anna Boncompagni
University of California, Irvine

Author for correspondence: Anna Boncompagni, anna.boncompagni@uci.edu

Abstract: The question of what Wittgenstein meant by "forms of life" has attracted a great deal of attention in the literature, yet it is an expression that Wittgenstein himself employs on only a relatively small number of occasions, and that he does not explicitly define. This Element gives a description of this concept that also explains Wittgenstein's reluctance to say much about it. A short historical introduction examines the origins and uses of the term in Wittgenstein's time. The Element then presents a survey of Wittgenstein's employment of it, and an overview of the literature. Finally, it offers a methodological reading of this notion, interpreting it as a conceptual tool in Wittgenstein's wider inquiries into the workings of our language.

Keywords: Wittgenstein, forms of life, language, language games, practices

ISBNs: 9781108931151 (PB), 9781108946513 (OC)
ISSNs: 2632-7112 (online), 2632-7104 (print)

Contents

1 Introduction

1.1 Overview

The question of what Ludwig Wittgenstein meant by "form of life" or "forms of life" (*Lebensform, Lebensformen*) has attracted a great deal of attention, although it is an expression that Wittgenstein himself employed only on a relatively small number of occasions. Since it seems to be at the core of Wittgenstein's later philosophy, one might wonder why he did not focus more explicitly on its meaning and significance. This Element aims to offer a clarification of this notion that also explains Wittgenstein's reluctance to be more explicit and straightforward about it.

The Element is structured into four parts: an introduction, two main sections, and a conclusion. In the introduction, I investigate the meaning(s) that *Lebensform* had at Wittgenstein's time. This investigation will provide at least a partial answer to the question posited. Indeed, the term was rather common at Wittgenstein's time, so much so that he probably did not think its meaning needed to be explicitly addressed. It was used both in the natural sciences and in philosophy, and it was used both to point to natural factors and features of certain species, among them the human species, and to highlight broadly cultural, social, and aesthetic elements that characterize and differentiate the various ways in which human beings organize and live their lives with each other. The concept of *Lebensform* was therefore not an "invention" of Wittgenstein but rather an idea that was already present in his cultural milieu and that he put to use for his specific purposes.

To illustrate such purposes, after the introduction, Section 2 will focus on the occasions on which Wittgenstein mentioned forms of life in his writings and lectures. Since the term appears only five times in the *Philosophical Investigations* (including both parts 1 and 2)[1] and a few times in other writings and lectures, the task of examining these occurrences in detail and tracing them back to their original formulations in Wittgenstein's manuscripts is not impossible. The analysis of the contexts in which *Lebensform* or *Lebensformen* appear

---

[1] Throughout this work, whenever I refer to the *Investigations* in general (without using abbreviations), I will be referring to the whole work as it was traditionally known, hence both part 1 and part 2. I will, however, use the abbreviations *PI* and *PPF*, following the use introduced by the fourth edition of the book (2009), when referring only to part 1 or only to part 2, respectively, and when quoting from or referring to specific remarks. In references to *PPF*, I will also add the section and page reference to the "old" *PI II* (from the third edition of the *Investigations*) in square brackets. For references to *Culture and Value*, I will use the 1998 edition, but add the reference to the 1980 edition in square brackets. For the abbreviations of Wittgenstein's works, see the bibliography. When referring to Wittgenstein's manuscripts and typescripts in the *Nachlass*, I use the standard classification (von Wright 1993) and quote from the Bergen Electronic Edition (BEE). Translations from the *Nachlass*, unless otherwise specified, are mine (often from Boncompagni 2015, where I benefited from the advice of Joachim Schulte).

will indeed help us understand the reasons motivating Wittgenstein's choice of this expression, what he connected it with, and what he was interested in highlighting. The variations that some passages went through between their original formulation and later versions also constitute a lens through which to examine the development of Wittgenstein's approach to certain issues. One point that will be addressed is the earliest occurrence of the term in his work, dating back to 1936: he first introduced *Lebensform* as a replacement for the word "culture." This change might suggest that there was something in "culture" that did not capture what he wanted to emphasize when he talked about forms of life. I will argue that unlike "forms of life," "culture" risks not capturing the practical, everyday, and ordinary aspects of the *things we do* when we use words. Another point that will emerge is Wittgenstein's views about the English translation of *Lebensform*, which, at least at some point, he thought should be "way of living." This translation, perhaps surprisingly, eliminates any talk of a "form" and instead emphasizes the activities, practices, and ways of doing in which our language games are embedded, which he elsewhere referred to as "the whole hurly burly" of life.

After this examination of Wittgenstein's remarks, in Section 3, the vast literature on Wittgenstein's notion of forms of life will be addressed. It might be surprising that so much has been written on a notion that he seldom employed, but I believe that the emphasis on it by many commentators is not misplaced. It will be fascinating to see with what purposes commentators stress the relevance of forms of life in Wittgenstein; in fact, interpretations diverge and point in different, sometimes opposing directions. To systematize the debate and add some clarity to it, I will identify some of the most discussed issues and some of the most relevant readings that have been offered. Some commentators, for instance, claim that Wittgenstein stresses the existence of basically one human form of life, while others emphasize his remarks about the different ways in which human beings, in their specific cultures and social settings, develop their own ways of living. Relatedly, some connect the human form of life to language in general, and some seem interested in considering the practices in which singular language games are embedded. Some interpreters offer a transcendental reading in which forms of life are to some extent the conditions of possibility for meaning and language. Others are inclined toward a naturalistic account that privileges biological and evolutionary aspects. The section includes early interpretations, such as those proposed by J. F. M. Hunter, Max Black, and Nicholas Gier; the influential work of Stanley Cavell, who distinguished between a vertical (biological) and a horizontal (cultural) dimension of the concept; and the transcendental readings proposed by, among others, Bernard Williams and Jonathan Lear. It also reviews more recent debates concerning such matters as whether Wittgenstein's interest in the plurality of forms of life entails a form of relativism, whether he should be considered a conservative thinker, and whether his reference to human practices makes him an empiricist and/or a naturalist.

In the fourth and concluding section, after recapping the most relevant insights gained from the former examinations and trying to map the survey of interpretations onto Wittgenstein's remarks, I develop my own take on this notion. To anticipate, I argue that the concept of forms of life functions as a methodological reminder for Wittgenstein. Wittgenstein was not providing an empirical explanation of what a form of life is. Instead, he was engaged in a grammatical investigation, highlighting the connections between speaking a language and being the particular animals that we are, belonging to communities that are held together by habit, education, norms, culture, and science. This explains Wittgenstein's seeming reluctance to say more about forms of life: his interest lay not in explaining forms of life in themselves but in making use of this conceptual tool in his wider inquiries into the workings of our language. Far from diminishing the significance of this notion, a methodological reading will highlight its centrality in Wittgenstein's overall project.

1.2 "Lebensformen" before Wittgenstein

Two sources are particularly helpful for grasping the way in which the term *Lebensform* was used before Wittgenstein and at his time and hence the meaning or meanings with which he was likely familiar. One source is Helmreich and Roosth's (2010) "keyword" account of the term "life-form", in which they examine how this term has been employed in natural philosophy and biology over the last two hundred years, beginning with its appearance in German as *Lebensform*. The second source is the *Historisches Wörterbuch der Philosophie* (Ritter, Gründer and Gabriel 2007). These two sources consider partly differing fields of research, with the former occasionally mentioning philosophy but certainly not focusing on it and the latter instead oriented toward philosophy. Combining them is therefore particularly useful.

Helmreich and Roosth note that according to the *Deutsche Wörterbuch*, the term *Lebensformen* first appeared in 1838 in the *Jenaer Literatur-Zeitung* with the meaning of "the physical properties of heavenly bodies and the life forms possible upon them" (2010: 31). In approximately the same period, a slightly different meaning is detectable in a work by Karl Friedrich Burdach on physiology in which the emphasis is not on the external environment but on the inner life forces of an organism: life-forms are described here as "self-organizing according to an inner principle" (Helmreich and Roosth 2010: 31; Burdach 1838). Both ideas, at that time, served to ground the possibility of constructing new classificatory schemes, in contrast with the prevalent view exemplified by Linnaeus' static taxonomy. This brings to mind Goethe's work on the morphology of plants, a work that Wittgenstein knew very well and that was in turn inspired by Kant's *Critique of Judgment* (more on Goethe and Kant soon). The same inspiration was at the origins of Johannes Müller's work. Müller, a physiologist and anatomist, teacher of Hermann von Helmholtz, Ernst Haeckel, and Louis Agassiz, between 1834 and 1840 published a piece titled (in Helmreich & Roosth's translation) "Concluding remarks on the variations of development in animal and human life forms on Earth" (Müller 1840).

Another set of thinkers who use the term *Lebensform*, including the philosopher Wilhelm von Humboldt and his younger brother, the naturalist Alexander von Humboldt, focused on the relationship between the organism and its environment and the role of habits and custom (Helmreich and Roosth 2010: 33). Recognizing their contribution requires backdating the first occurrences of the term with respect to the *Deutsche Wörterbuch*. Wilhelm von Humboldt in fact talks of *Lebensform* as early as 1824, treating it as a synonym of custom or culture. His brother Alexander generalizes this notion to the organic world, including plants. From Helmreich and Roosth's article, we also learn that Alexander von Humboldt influenced Charles Darwin and that Darwin's grandfather, Erasmus Darwin, had already used the term "form of life" (in English) at the end of the eighteenth and beginning of the nineteenth century.

The legacy of the two von Humboldts extends to Ernst Haeckel's very popular works, including his *Generelle Morphologie der Organismen* (1866) and *Natürliche Schöpfungsgeschichte* (1868), which had multiple editions and contributed significantly to spreading Darwin's work in the German-speaking world. Haeckel is especially remembered for his idea that ontogeny recapitulates phylogeny, that is, the life of the organism recapitulates the evolution of the species.

The English expressions "life-form" and "form of life," sometimes with reference to life on other worlds, became common in the mid- and late nineteenth century in both the United Kingdom and the United States (Helmreich and Roosth 2010: 36–37).

From other more philosophy-oriented sources, including the *Historisches Wörterbuch der Philosophie* (Ritter et al. 2007), we learn that Friedrich Schleiermacher uses the word *Lebensform* as early as his lectures on psychology in 1830 while considering the relationship between the individual and society (Schleiermacher 1862).[2] Wilhelm Wundt, considered the founder of modern

---

[2]   The lectures were given between 1818 and 1834. According to Hacker (2015: 2), Schleiermacher used the term *Lebensform* as a synonym of *Lebenstypus*, with the meaning "personal character formation in relation to society."

experimental psychology, investigates *Lebensformen* in connection with customs and morality in his *Ethik*, first published in 1886. He differentiates between specific forms of life, that is, customs in which individual needs (food, dwelling, clothing, work) are met, forms of "intercourse" (the labor contract, play, good manners, salutation), social forms of life (family, tribal unions, the state, the legal system), and humanistic forms of life (friendship, hospitality, charity), which are attained through agreement (*Übereinstimmung*) in the spiritual qualities of human beings (Wundt 1908; see in particular vol. 1, chapter 3).[3]

In the twentieth century, the *Historisches Wörterbuch* mentions Eduard Spranger, whose book *Lebensformen* (first published in 1914 and then revised in 1921) was widely read at Wittgenstein's time (Spranger 1921). Spranger was a student of Wilhelm Dilthey, and his work can be considered a development of Dilthey's conception of life. Spranger classified six basic ideal-typical forms of individuality, or characters (his book was indeed translated into English as *Types of Men*). These different, alternative, even rival types of minds (for instance, the military, the contemplative, and the artistic mind) reflect alternative *Lebensformen*, modes or styles or ways of life, each characterized by its own basic ethical systems or structures of values: theoretical, economic, aesthetic, social, political, and religious forms of life. The lineage from Spranger to Wittgenstein is generally acknowledged in the Wittgensteinian literature. One of the first commentaries on Wittgenstein's *Philosophical Investigations*, Hallett (1977: 88–89), partly following Toulmin (1969: 71), directly connects Wittgenstein's notion to the influence of Spranger's book. Baker and Hacker (1980: 136), instead, claim that there is no reason to associate Wittgenstein's use of this term with Spranger's work.[4]

Spranger also worked on developmental psychology and on adolescent life, other fields in which the notion of forms of life seems to have been in use. For instance, Herman Nohl, whose research developed in strict contact with both Dilthey and Spranger, investigates the way in which education is influenced and shaped by cultural backgrounds and worldviews and mentions *Lebensformen* in his *Charakter und Schicksal* (1938).[5]

---

[3] Among the thinkers of the nineteenth century, we should add Arthur Schopenhauer, who uses the expression *Form des Lebens* on a few occassions in *Die Welt als Wille und Vorstellung* (1819). He is not among the authors listed in the *Historisches Wörterbuch*, presumably, because he does not employ the word *Lebensformen* (I will say something more about *Lebensform* and *Form des Leben* in Section 2).

[4] Here and elsewhere, I am referring to the first edition of volume I of Baker and Hacker's commentary; some parts that are of interest for the notion of forms of life were in fact not included in the 2005 revised edition.

[5] Interestingly, Nohl was a relative of Wittgenstein, having married his cousin, the pianist Bertha Oser. Bertha was the daughter of Wittgenstein's aunt Josephine ("Aunt Fine" in family letters; see McGuinness 2019: 150, 154–56). See Wittgenstein's family tree in Avins' (2014: 225) study.

Another author worth mentioning is Alfred Wechsler, who wrote under the pseudonym of W. Fred and published a monograph titled *Lebensformen: Anmerkungen über die Technik des gesellschaftlichen Lebens* (*Forms of Life: Remarks on the Techniques of Social Life*; Fred 1905). This work is analyzed in depth by Margit Gaffal (2011).[6] Topics included among "the techniques of social life" are good manners, personalities, appearance and reality, fashion, marriage and love, conversation, habits of eating, sports, reading, and traveling. One aspect underlined by Fred/Wechsler is the emergence of new forms of life, for instance, that of the "cosmopolitans," who contributed to spreading modern ways of living to more traditional small towns. As Gaffal (2011) notes, Fred/Wechsler warns against adopting a new form of life without reflection just because it is new. A form of life, he claims, has the "right" to exist and to be followed only "if it coincides with the deep laws of humanity" (quoted in Gaffal 2011: 61). A form of life therefore also connects to a deeper level and must be grounded, ultimately, in human nature. This aspect will also emerge in the Wittgensteinian notion. Another aspect that will resurface is the emphasis on the implicitness of forms of life: a form of life is basically a set of implicit, tacit know-hows that are manifested in the naturalness of people's behavior in various, often complex social contexts. Fred/Wechsler praises the English over the German form of life precisely because it remains more tacit.[7] The relationship between the individual and the social rules embedded in forms of life is also an aspect considered by Fred/Wechsel, according to whom individuals cannot "make" their own forms of life but must to a certain extent adapt to the existent form of life in which they live.[8]

The series of monographs published at the beginning of the twentieth century with "forms of life" in their title does not end here. Another representative of the collection is *Lebensform und Lebensfunktionen der Rede* by the linguist Hermann Ammann (1928), a study of human speech that brings into focus the "lively" nature of language and its relationship with forms of life, analyzing, for instance, primitive forms of syntax such as exclamations in connection to elementary speech acts, such as cursing, congratulating, or blessing (cf. Padilla Gálvez and Gaffal 2011: 13). In 1919, Dutch linguist and historian of culture Johan Huizinga published *Waning of Middle Ages: A Study of the Forms*

---

[6] See also Hacker 2015: 2–3; Haller 2014: 133–34.

[7] In his review of this book, Hugo von Hofmannsthal underlined how forms of life "say without words what no one would agree if said with words and concepts" (cited in Abreu e Silva Netu 2011: 97).

[8] Compare Wittgenstein: "The solution of the problem you see in life is a way of living which makes what is problematic disappear. / The fact that life is problematic means that your life does not fit life's shape (*Form des Leben*). So you must change your life, & once it fits the shape, what is problematic will disappear" (*CV*: 31 [27]).

of Life, Thought and Art in France and the Netherlands in the 14th and 15th Centuries (translated into both German and English in 1924), in which he talks of forms of life in terms of the spirit of an epoch that is manifested in practices, customs, and habits (Huizinga 1924; cf. Abreu e Silva Netu 2011: 90).

Finally, other thinkers who deserve at least a mention are the architect and designer Adolf Loos (with whom Wittgenstein was familiar), for his insistence on the fact that the design of an object must connect to the "forms of culture" and manners of life in which it is used (Janik and Toulmin 1973: 230); Karl and Charlotte Bühler (friends of Wittgenstein's sister Margaret), who offer important contributions to developmental psychology and linguistics (Toulmin 1969: 71); Alfred Adler, physician and psychotherapist, who analyzes children's development based on the "form of life" that the child acquires during infancy (Padilla Gálvez and Gaffal 2011: 10); the philosopher and theologian Heinrich Scholz, for his work on religious forms of life (Ritter et al. 2007); and Paul Ernst, for his distinction between "organic" and "inorganic" (bourgeois) forms of life and his criticism of the latter (Nyíri 1981).

Statistics show that the use of the term *"Lebensform"* peaked between 1930 and 1940 – precisely when Wittgenstein started to use it – and remained high thereafter (Floyd 2018: 61).

1.3 Goethe and Spengler: Methodological Concerns

In the Wittgensteinian literature, two authors receive particular consideration for their influence on the development of the Wittgensteinian version of the notion of forms of life: Goethe and Spengler. In my view, they are especially important to the methodological role that this notion assumes in Wittgenstein's work.

The Goethean and, by way of Goethe, broadly Kantian influence is emphasized, among others, by Abreu e Silva Netu (2011: 78–83), who highlights the intertwinement of a subjective and a cosmological dimension in Kant's perspective on the notion of form (especially in the Third Critique) and connects it to Goethe's method of comparative morphology (Goethe 1946 [1790]). The indebtedness of Wittgenstein's own method of surveyable representation (or synoptic representation) and the use of "objects of comparison" (*PI* §§122, 130) to Goethe's morphology is acknowledged by many (see, for instance, Schulte 1984, 2017; Andronico 1999; Breithaupt et al. 2003). Wittgenstein is indeed explicit about the similarities between his aims and methods and Goethe's views. In commenting on the latter's conception of the "original plant," in which the point is not so much to explain a plant's temporal development à la Darwin as to offer "a plan" in which it is possible to group the organs of plants on the basis of their similarities "as if around some natural center," Wittgenstein and Waismann explain, "This is precisely what we are doing here. We are collating one form of language with its environment, or transforming it in imagination so as to gain a view of the whole space in which the structure of our language has its being" (Waismann 1965: 81).[9] Even if Wittgenstein and Waismann are not talking about forms of life at that time, Wittgenstein's slightly later notion of forms of life and the way in which he uses it resonates significantly with these words.

However, the thinker who is most often mentioned as being at the origins of the Wittgensteinian notion is Oswald Spengler, with whose *Der Untergang des Abendlandes* (*The Decline of the West*), published in 1918 (first volume) and 1922 (second volume), Wittgenstein was very familiar. In *The Decline of the West*, Spengler deals with cultures and civilizations as organisms with their lifecycle. He argues that a civilization is the destiny or final stage of a culture once it stops growing internally and creatively and starts expanding externally and rigidly. Spengler uses the expression *Lebensform* several times in connection with both the human form of life in general and specific historical forms of life (socialism, for example). The method of Spengler's inquiry owes much to Goethe, although he applies it to history rather than to natural organisms. Rejecting an idea of history based on the study of causes and effects, Spengler wants to understand cultures and their developments by looking closely at their physiognomies. He examines the analogies in forms between different epochs in the same way in which one can examine the analogies between the organs in different living beings, focusing on their functions and on the relations of the parts to the whole. To some extent echoing Haeckel's idea of ontogeny recapitulating phylogeny, but without its evolutionistic commitment, Spengler claims that the grandiose history of civilizations is *morphologically* in relationship with the microscopic history of an animal or a flower.

The relevance of Spengler to the development of the Wittgensteinian notion is emphasized, among others, by Baker and Hacker's (1980: 136–37) influential commentary on *PI*, in which these passages from *The Decline of the West* are brought up as an example:

> [T]he words *History* and *Nature* are here employed ... in a quite different and hitherto unusual sense. These words comprise *possible* modes of understanding, of comprehending the totality of knowledge ... as a homogeneous, spiritualized, well ordered *world-picture* .... The possibilities that we have

---

[9] I am attributing this to Wittgenstein as well as Waismann, although the quotation is from the latter's *Principles of Linguistic Philosophy* (Waismann 1965: 81); indeed, I think that these lines capture Wittgenstein's own views at the time he was collaborating with Waismann in the early 1930s. See also *VW*: 311.

of possessing an "outer world" that reflects and attests our proper existence are infinitely numerous and exceedingly heterogeneous . . . . One condition of this higher world-consciousness is the possession of *language*, meaning thereby not mere human utterance but a culture-language.[10]

While taking inspiration from Goethe and Spengler, Wittgenstein, however, does not refrain from criticizing them. His point is that they were not able to keep the method and object of inquiry separated. He claims that there is a risk in using "prototypes" or objects of comparison without an explicit awareness that these are only prototypes and objects of comparison: the risk of *wanting* to find the prototype in the phenomenon. There is a "prejudice"[11] in Spengler, Wittgenstein claims; in particular (*CV*: 30 [26 27], *PI* §131), he should have realized the importance of keeping the method and object of inquiry separate. Even more, he should have realized that he was inventing a method rather than discovering the laws that govern the history of cultures and civilizations (*CV*: 31 [26–27]; Hacker 2015: 3).[12] We will see how this methodological awareness plays out in Wittgenstein's notion of forms of life in the concluding section. Before that, however, we will look more closely at Wittgenstein's own remarks on forms of life and the most relevant interpretations in the literature.

To conclude on the uses of *Lebensform* before Wittgenstein and at Wittgenstein's time, as the short survey just presented shows, Wittgenstein cannot be said to have "invented" the notion of forms of life: "[T]his was just one of those cultural commonplaces that did not need explaining" (Janik and Toulmin 1973: 230). Additionally, it is noteworthy that in the uses of *Lebensform* that were common at his time, it is possible to identify both a biological dimension, in which the object of investigation is a living organism and its place in a physical environment, and a cultural and definitely human dimension, in which the connection between the individual and the collective instead assumes prominence (we will see in the next sections that both aspects also emerge in Wittgenstein's writings). Finally, the two authors who seem to have been particularly relevant for the development of Wittgenstein's approach, Goethe and Spengler, both pointed toward a methodological employment of the notions of form and forms of life, even if, in Wittgenstein's view, neither was able to keep faith to this intuition.

---

[10] Spengler's expression translated here as "culture-language" is *Kultursprache*; see Spengler 1919: 80.

[11] *Ungerechtigkeit*, also injustice, distortion, unfairness.

[12] On Wittgenstein's criticism of Spengler, see also Andronico 1999 and Schulte 2018. On the relevance of Spengler for Wittgenstein more generally, see also von Wright 1981 and Cavell 1988.

2 Forms of Life in Wittgenstein's Work

2.1 Overview

This section examines the occurrences of the terms *Lebensform* and Lebensformen in Wittgenstein's published writings, his lectures, and his manuscripts. Since Wittgenstein did not use these terms many times, it is feasible to consider all the occurrences of this expression in his work (some of which are in fact reformulations of the same remark).[13] By examining not only the best-known remarks from the *Investigations* but also their earlier formulations, as well as other remarks from other sources, it will be possible to obtain an overview of the different shades of meaning that this notion suggests.

This section is therefore largely exegetical and relies on a number of quotations from Wittgenstein's work. I will limit references to the secondary literature in order to approach Wittgenstein's words without being guided by preconceived interpretations or frameworks (as far as possible). The analysis of the most relevant readings that have been defended in the literature will be the focus of Section 3.

I will proceed by reviewing clusters of remarks that seem to inhabit the same semantic area and were written in approximately the same period. Because the remarks that appear in the *Investigations* are better known, for each cluster, I will start from those remarks, trace them back to their original formulation when possible, and extend the analysis to similar notes from other writings. The three semantic areas that we will examine relate broadly to the following themes:

(1) Language games and the activities of life (starting from *PI* §§19 and 23, remarks from 1936–7)
(2) Agreement and following a rule (starting from *PI* §241, remarks from 1938 and the first half of the 1940s)
(3) Forms of life as the "given" (starting from *PPF* §§1 and 345 [i 148, xi 192], remarks from after the Second World War).

Wittgenstein uses both *Lebensform* and *Lebensformen* in his writings, speaking both in the singular and the plural. Although some commentators have focused on this distinction (see Section 3), I do not think it is particularly significant, and I will therefore not use it as a criterion for distinguishing groups of remarks. Wittgenstein also occasionally uses *Form des Lebens*, whose difference from *Lebensform* is not immediately apparent in English ("form of our life" or "form of one's life" could possibly be good translations).

---

[13] At least, these are all the occurrences I am aware of.

For the sake of keeping the analysis limited and because I think that at least sometimes when using *Form des Lebens*, Wittgenstein is giving more importance to the notion of "form" in the sense of "shape," I will focus on *Lebensform*, touching on *Form des Lebens* only when it appears as a variant of *Lebensform*.[14]

2.2 Cluster 1: Language Games and Activities of Life

The first remark that includes "*Lebensform*" in the *Investigations* is the following:

> It is easy to imagine a language consisting only of orders and reports in battle. – Or a language consisting only of questions and expressions for answering Yes and No – and countless other things. – And to imagine a language means to imagine a form of life [*Lebensform*]. (*PI* §19)

This remark belongs to a longer reflection on the well-known example, put forth in *PI* §2, of the builder and the assistant who use what Wittgenstein calls a "complete primitive language" consisting only of the words "block," "pillar," "slab," and "beam." When a slab is needed, the builder calls out "Slab!" and the assistant brings it. In *PI* §18, Wittgenstein invites the reader not to consider this imaginary language incomplete, as we would not have considered our own language incomplete before – for instance – the symbolism of chemistry was introduced into it. Our language, he continues, is like an ancient city, with old and new streets and houses, including newer suburbs with straight and regular streets (the symbolism of chemistry): we would not say that the city was incomplete before it included the suburbs. Similarly, the primitive language of the builder and the assistant should not be considered incomplete before the introduction of other elements. The possibility of extending language is always open and does not entail a language being incomplete before the extension. It is at this juncture that "form of life" is introduced. The language of the builder and assistant is an imaginary language consisting only of imperatives about bringing objects; similarly, one can imagine a language consisting only of orders and reports or questions and yes/no answers, and so forth. Imagining such a language is possible if one can imagine a context in which it makes sense. Imagining the language of the builder and assistant, Wittgenstein suggests, means imagining the activities and practices in which such language is embedded: it means imagining its form of life.

---

[14] Two examples of the use of *Forms des Lebens* are *CV*: 31 [27], from MS 118: 17r–17v (1937) – "The fact that life is problematic means that your life does not fit life's shape [*die Form des Lebens*]. So you must change your life, and once it fits the shape, what is problematic will disappear" (cf. *RFM*: 132) – and MS 127: 128 (1944) – "Even the devil in hell has *one* form of life [*Form des Lebens*]" (see Schulte 2010, from which I am also borrowing the translation, for an analysis).

The next part of *PI* §19 confronts the temptation to consider "Slab!" an abbreviated form of "Bring me a slab!" and the consequent problems arising from the meanings of the two expressions and how they relate to each other (an issue that is not our concern here).

Let us trace *PI* §19 back to its earlier formulations. In the early version of *PI* (MS 142 and the typed version, TS 220), the remark is almost identical to its final formulation, the only difference being that "*sich*" appears twice instead of once in the last sentence.[15] The organization of the paragraphs is slightly different, with the lines on form of life being part of what is now *PI* §18 and the rest of what is now *PI* §19 constituting an independent remark.

However, something more interesting emerges when we examine the first formulation of this idea from the *Brown Book*. In this context, Wittgenstein invites the reader to imagine a situation, a tribe, or a culture in which the names for colors are arranged differently, for instance, with a common name for green and red and another common name for yellow and blue. One can imagine this by supposing, say, that in this hypothetical tribe or culture, there are two castes, one always wearing green and red and the other yellow and blue. Similarly, it is possible to imagine a culture in which light blue and dark blue are not both labeled "blue" but have different names, such as (Wittgenstein's example) "Cambridge" and "Oxford"; a member of this "tribe," if asked what a dark and a light blue patch have in common, would reply, "Nothing" (*BBB*: 134–35). Here, Wittgenstein is making the same point as that in *PI* §19: it is about the embeddedness of a language in a form of life and the possibility of imagining such a language by making up a fictitious form of life in which it would "work." However, what is interesting here is that he does *not* mention forms of life:

> Imagine a use of language (a culture) in which there was a common name for green and red on the one hand and yellow and blue on the other. . . . We could also easily imagine a language (and that means again a culture) in which there existed no common expression for light blue and dark blue. (*BBB*: 134–35)

The role that in *PI* §19 is played by "forms of life" is played here by "culture."

The introduction of the term "form of life" in this passage – the first time Wittgenstein uses it, to my knowledge – occurs in the second part of MS 115, which is an attempt to revise and translate the *Brown Book* into German.[16] Here, we can read the following:

---

[15] "*Und sich eine Sprache vorstellen heisst, sich eine Lebensform vorstellen*" (*PU*: 221). For early versions of the *Investigations*, I am using the critical-genetic edition edited by Schulte (Wittgenstein 2001; abbr. *PU*).

[16] Wittgenstein was probably working on Francis Skinner's handwritten copy of the *Brown Book* rather than the version that was later published (TS 310) (cf. Pichler and Smith 2013: 311, n. 3;

Let us imagine a linguistic use (a culture) in which there is a common name for green and red, and one for blue and yellow. ... I could also think of a language (and this means again a form of life [*eine Lebensform/Forms des Lebens*]), which establishes a chasm between dark red and light red.

(MS 115: 238–39)

It is at this point, then, in trying to revise and translate the *Brown Book* into German, that Wittgenstein realizes he does not want to use "culture" and that "*Lebensform*" better captures his intended meaning.

The first page of this part of MS 115 is dated "End of August 1936"; on the last page, Wittgenstein gives up the project of translating the *Brown Book*, saying that it is "not worth anything." Later that year, he starts writing the early version of *PI* (MS 142), in which, as we saw, he employs the term *Lebensform*. It is plausible to argue, then, that this moment in time, coinciding with the introduction of the concept of forms of life, marks a turning point in Wittgenstein's trajectory, confirming the significance of this notion.

Why did Wittgenstein abandon "culture" in favor of "form of life"? One reason might be that, given that Spengler's book was widely known and discussed in the German-speaking world, talking of *Kultur* would somewhat too directly connect Wittgenstein's reflection to the Spenglerian notion of *Kultur*, which was seen as in opposition to *Zivilisation*. Perhaps Wittgenstein did not want to refer to this dialectic when he was reflecting on the relevance of cultural environments to understand the nature of language. Another related but broader reason might be that a culture is often thought of as something related to a complex, specialized if not theoretical form of knowledge that only the "acculturated" members of society possess. In contrast, the Wittgensteinian reflection seems directed toward the everyday shared and unreflective background of practices and know-how that is the natural environment of language, a form of agreement or consensus manifested in human activities that is *presupposed* by language and culture itself (cf. Baker and Hacker 1980: 137).[17]

A couple of thinkers might have had a role in Wittgenstein's switch from "culture" to "forms of life." One is the economist Piero Sraffa, a close friend of Wittgenstein. Sraffa's role in Wittgenstein's abandoning the perspective of the *Tractatus* in the early 1930s and the episode of the gesture that Wittgenstein

---

Gibson and Mahony 2020: 28, 75). However, this part of the Skinner manuscript is identical to the *Brown Book*. I thank David Stern for his help with this.

[17] Note that Wittgenstein does use "culture" in connection with language games slightly later, but in a remark concerned with aesthetic judgments, hence precisely with an expert and specialized form of knowledge: "The words we call expressions of aesthetic judgement play a very complicated role, but a very definite role, in what we call a culture of a period. To describe their use or to describe what you mean by a cultured taste, you have to describe a culture. ... What belongs to a language game is a whole culture" (*LC*: 8 [1938]).

himself identified as decisive are well known (Malcolm 2001: 58). However, less studied is the extent to which Sraffa's criticism continued to contribute to the development of Wittgenstein's most important ideas. Wittgenstein himself acknowledges the relevance of Sraffa to his work. In the preface of the *Investigations*, he notably affirms that he owes to Sraffa's stimulus "the most fruitful ideas" contained in the book (*PI*: 4). One of these "most fruitful ideas" may be that of forms of life. Although no direct connection is textually traceable, the introduction of this notion in MS 115ii and then *PI* §19 is tied to the Wittgensteinian method of imagining elementary "primitive" language games, and this method strongly resembles the method Sraffa employed in his *Production of Commodities by Means of Commodities* (1960). The first chapter of Sraffa's book (just like the *Brown Book*) begins with a hypothetical "extremely simple society," a subsistence economic system consisting of only a few elementary components without surplus; in the following chapters, Sraffa introduces new variables (Engelmann 2013 170, n. 41). Correspondence between Sraffa and Wittgenstein also emphasizes the importance that both assigned to having "particular cases" as their starting point (see, for instance, McGuinness 2012: 196). Note that even if Wittgenstein leaves aside the idea of proceeding systematically (and slightly pedantically) from simple cases to more complex ones, as he did in the *Brown Book*, in the *Investigations*, he still proposes, on several occasions, elementary and "primitive examples," sometimes suggesting ways to complexify them.[18]

Another figure who might have had a relevant role at this stage is Alan Turing. In particular, Wittgenstein's reading of Turing's paper "On Computable Numbers, with an Application to the *Entscheidungsproblem*" (Turing 1936–7), the conversations between the two, and possibly also some discussions with the mathematician Alister Watson on Turing's work before Turing's paper was published might have contributed to pushing Wittgenstein toward a conception of logic and language as deeply human, embedded in human activities, and utterly unconceivable in abstraction from them (Floyd 2016, 2018, 2020). Far from being a computational reductionist, as he has often been portrayed, Turing was in fact interested in and worked on the *human* foundation of logic and on machines as they can be *used* by human beings. As

---

[18] On the methodological convergences between Wittgenstein and Sraffa, see Arena 2013. In general terms, both Wittgenstein and Sraffa affirm the primacy of social contexts and practices over individual inner states and preferences, whether for the determination and understanding of the meanings of words (philosophy) or for the determination and explanation of prices (economics). In this sense, Sraffa's criticism of the neoclassical model focused on individual preferences abstracted from a social context finds a philosophical counterpart in Wittgenstein's criticism of private language and his identification of forms of life as the environment of language games (Davis 1988: 34–36; Davis 1993).

Floyd writes, "Within the framework of logic, Turing showed that an order can only be followed in a context. Wittgenstein spells out in his later philosophy the idea that *Regelmäßigkeit* [regularity] only makes sense in the context of a *Lebensform*" (Floyd 2020: 127).

To recapitulate regarding the first mention of *Lebensformen* in Wittgenstein's work, this notion replaced the concept of culture; it was meant to capture the embeddedness of language in the activities and practices of life; and it signaled an anthropological attention to how language and logic are *practiced* in every-day contexts. Sraffa and Turing were most likely relevant for the development of Wittgenstein's ideas on this subject.

The second remark on forms of life in the *Investigations* relates broadly to the same themes.

> But how many kinds of sentence are there? Say assertion, question, and command? – There are *countless* kinds; countless different kinds of use of all the things we call "signs", "words", "sentences". And this diversity is not something fixed, given once for all; but new types of language, new language-games, as we may say, come into existence, and others become obsolete and get forgotten. (We can get a *rough picture* of this from the changes in mathematics.)
>
> The word "language-*game*" is used here to emphasize the fact that the *speaking* of language is part of an activity, or of a form of life [*Lebensform*]. (*PI* §23)

This remark follows a train of thought generated in *PI* §19 (the passage just examined) and dealing with different kinds of sentences. Remark 22 of *PI* is on Frege's notion of assertion: placing it in this context implies suggesting that assertion is only one among many kinds of sentences, in no way privileged with respect to others. Remark 23 of *PI* indeed affirms that there are "countless" ways of using signs, words, and sentences. In the second part of this remark (omitted in the quotation), Wittgenstein expands on the notion of language games by listing examples that include giving and obeying orders, describing, following instructions, reporting events, forming and testing hypotheses, reading a story, acting in a play, singing, telling jokes, solving an arithmetical problem, translating, thanking, greeting, praying, and others.[19] This remark therefore establishes a strict connection between language games (the *speaking* of a language, as opposed to language as an abstract entity) and forms of life, in this case seemingly equating a form of life with an "activity." The remark ends with the comment that it is interesting to compare this multiplicity of linguistic

---

[19] The notion of language games is introduced in the *Investigations* in *PI* §7, but Wittgenstein had already used it in earlier notes (see, for instance, *BT*: 156–62; *BBB*: 17, 81).

tools and ways of using them "with what logicians have said about the structure of language, [including] the author of the *Tractatus logico-Philosophicus*."

In the following remark, *PI* §24, Wittgenstein further explains that overlooking the variety of language games can lead one to see, for instance, questions or cries for help as modifications or special cases of descriptions. In addition, in *PI* §25, he clarifies that language games such as giving orders, telling stories, or asking questions belong to our natural history as do other natural behaviors, for instance, walking, eating, or playing.

The part of *PI* §23 that includes the term *Lebensform* is already in the early prewar version of *PI* (MS 142, late 1936), although the expression *Lebensform* itself appears to be an addition. These lines are on page 20, after the series of examples of language games, with the indication "*Zu S. [Seite] 19*," "to page 19" (see MS 142: 19–20, or *PU*: 42). The words "*oder Lebensform*" were visibly added afterward. The remark begins in the familiar way – "the word 'language-*game*' is used here to emphasize the fact that the *speaking* of a language is ... " – and then shows alternative versions:

... a determinate process [variant: part] of a form of activity [added variant: of an activity or of a form of life].

... a determinate process [variant: part] of an activity [added: or of a form of life].[20]

It seems fair to hypothesize that Wittgenstein is here formulating this remark for the first time (which explains the uncertainties). In the typed version of MS 142, TS 220 (1937), Wittgenstein chooses the formulation that eventually finds its way to the final version of *PI* ("the speaking of language is part of an activity, or of a form of life," TS 220: 16).[21]

Another interesting document regarding these two first occurrences of *Lebensform* in *PI* is TS 226, a 1939 translation into English of one of the prewar versions of *PI*, made by Rush Rhees and revised by Wittgenstein. Wittgenstein's revisions are clearly visible here because they are handwritten on the typescript. Wittgenstein does not intervene in Rhees' translation of the first remark, which is as follows: "And to imagine a language means to imagine a *way of living*" (TS 226: 10; my emphasis). In the second remark, Wittgenstein makes minor corrections, resulting in the following: "The expression 'language game' is used

---

[20] German: *ein Teilvorgang* [variant: *Teil*] *ist einer Form der Tätigkeit* [added: *oder einer Lebensform*]// *ein Teilvorgang* [variant: *Teil*] *einer Tätigkeit* [added: *oder Lebensform*] *ist* (MS 142: 20).

[21] The line of reasoning from Frege's assertion to the multiplicity of language games, as well as many of the examples of language games that Wittgenstein provides in *PI* §23, had already appeared in previous writings (see in particular *BT*: 157–63; *BBB* 67–68), but the notion of forms of life had not.

here to emphasize that the speaking of the language is part of an activity, part of *a way of living of human beings*" (TS 226: 15; my emphasis). *A way of living*, not a form of life: this was how Wittgenstein wanted (or at least accepted) *Lebensform* to be translated into English.

What does this document tell us concerning the meaning Wittgenstein attributed to *Lebensform*? First, it seems that the reference to a "form" is not considered so important (at least in the remarks from this period). Wittgenstein apparently did not intend to point to formal characteristics of our life, such as a model or a structure inherent in it. Second, in referring to the way in which human beings live, he apparently was interested in the ways in which humans conduct their activities; in connecting this to the multifarious language games in which we are constantly engaged, he was contextualizing language use within everyday practices and establishing a nexus between the meanings of our words and practical contexts of use.[22] However, in using *Lebensform* rather than *Lebensweise, Lebensart*, or *Art des Lebens* in German (expressions more akin to "way of life" and "lifestyle" that he also used),[23] Wittgenstein was most likely pointing at something that goes somewhat deeper than a lifestyle or a fashion.

This is confirmed by a set of remarks that were written in October 1937:

> I want to say: it is characteristic of our language that the foundation [*Grund*] on which it grows consists in steady ways of living [*fester Lebensformen*], regular ways of acting.
> ... We have an idea of which ways of living [*Lebensformen*] are primitive, and which could only have developed out of these. We believe that the simplest plough existed before the complicated one.
> The simple form (and that is the prototype [*Urform*]) of the cause-effect game is determining the cause, not doubting. (*PO*: 397)

Here, Wittgenstein is concerned with the "game" of identifying the causes of phenomena, a reflection stimulated by Bertrand Russell's paper "The Limits of Empiricism" (1935–6). In this context, he speaks of foundations, bases, primitive forms, simple forms, and prototypes (Goethe resonates here): a way of living plays a foundational, grounding role for the development of language and of language games.[24] These remarks anticipate Wittgenstein's later reflections in *OC*, in which he is concerned with the primacy of certainty over doubt and

---

[22] This also emerges in Wittgenstein's Whewell's Court Lectures from 1938–41, in which he often refers to ways of life, practices, and facts of our life (see, for instance, *WCL*: 230–32, 244). See also *LC*: 11.

[23] See, for instance, *RFM*: 335 – "Language, I should like to say, relates to a *way* of living" – where he emphasized "*way*" [Lebens<u>weise</u> in the original manuscript, MS 164: 98] in order to contrast established practices with something that happens only once.

[24] See also *PO*: 377, 397, where Wittgenstein speaks of "the basic form [*Grundform*]" of the game.

with the basic presuppositions, assumptions, or commitments that ground and orient our practices as well as our personal lives.

2.3 Cluster 2: Agreement and Rules

A relatively early use of "forms of life", scarcely considered in the literature, will allow us to connect the topic of certainty to the second cluster of remarks, which is broadly focused on the themes of consensus, agreement, custom, and rules.

This is a remark on fundamental religious convictions from 1938:

> Why shouldn't one form of life culminate in an utterance of belief in a Last Judgment? But I couldn't either say "Yes" or "No" to the statement that there will be such a thing. Nor "Perhaps", nor "I'm not sure."[25] (*LC*: 58)

What associates these lines with the remarks just examined is the seemingly grounding role played by such a religious conviction in the life of a believer (cf. Pritchard 2018). A conviction of this kind is not like an empirical belief that can be proven right or wrong by checking whether it matches the facts; arguments and disagreements about religious convictions are different from ordinary arguments and disagreements. Similarly, an agreement about something relating to our form of life is different from and deeper than an agreement in *opinions*. We come here to the third remark on forms of life in the *Investigations*:

> So you are saying that human agreement decides what is true and what is false? – What is true or false is what human beings *say*; and it is in their *language* that human beings agree. This is agreement not in opinions, but rather in form of life [*Lebensform*]. (*PI* §241)

These lines appear at the end of a *PI* section in which Wittgenstein is working on following a rule. In particular, Wittgenstein is focusing on the "matter of course" with which we generally follow rules in well-established practices, such as mathematics. Indeed, in *PI* §240, Wittgenstein observes that disputes about whether a rule has been followed normally do not arise among mathematicians because "this belongs to the scaffolding from which our language operates." It is at this point that Wittgenstein's imaginary interlocutor challenges him, asking whether in this view, in the end, it is human agreement that decides what is true and false. Wittgenstein's answer does not deny that following a rule is a matter of human agreement but does deny that such agreement is an agreement in opinions. One cannot *be of the opinion* that (say) 2 and 2 is 4 or that 1,000 and 2 is 1,002. However, one can belong to a form of life whose members agree on 2 and 2 being 4 and 1,000 and 2 being 1,002. This is an agreement both in

---

[25] Note that this lecture was given in English, and Wittgenstein speaks here of forms of life, not ways of living.

definitions and procedures and in judgments, both in the methods of measurements and in the results of measurements (*PI* §242; cf. *RFM*: 342–43), but *not* an agreement in opinions. Where does this idea about agreement come from?

Remarks §§241 and 242 of *PI* represent the conclusion of a long reflection in which Wittgenstein distinguishes and at the same time highlights the interconnectedness between rules and applications (practices, actions). In mentioning forms of life in this circumstance and distinguishing the concept from opinion, he suggests that forms of life have the fundamentality of rules, but at the same time, just like rules, they are permeable to slow changes brought about by the ways in which they are ordinarily practiced. Wittgenstein's later metaphor of the river and the riverbed of thought (*OC* §§96–99) illustrates, I think, the same point. there is a distinction between the movements of the waters and the (possibly imperceptible) movements of the riverbed, even if the course of the riverbed itself can slowly change in response to changes in the flow of the waters. The distinction between the movements of the riverbed and of its waters is of the same kind as the distinctions between rule and action and between forms of life and opinions.

If we wonder when *PI* §241 was written, we find that it does not belong to the early, prewar version of *PI*. Early formulations of this remark are present in manuscripts 124, 129, and 180. In the first one (from 1944), the wording is slightly different, and there are some variants:

> So you are saying, that human agreement determines [*bestimmt*; variant: decides, *entscheidet*] what is true and false [variant: right and wrong, *richtig und unrichtig*]?
> Right and wrong can only be found in thinking, that is, in the expression of thoughts; and the expression of thoughts, language, is common to all people. It is in a form of life that they agree (not in an opinion). (MS 124: 212–13)

The remark is here preceded by early formulations of what are now *PI* §§210–13, about continuing a series.

The formulation in MS 180 (dated 1944 or 1945) is approximately the same, as is the sequence of remarks (MS 180: 4v–5r).

In MS 129 (late 1944–beginning of 1945), the remark is instead practically identical to *PI* §241 and is preceded by what are now *PI* §§210, 211, 217, 212, and 213 (see pp. 33–35). I would like to draw attention to *PI* §217 in particular. This is a well-known remark in which Wittgenstein affirms,

> Once I have exhausted the justifications, I have reached bedrock, and my spade is turned. Then I am inclined to say: "This is simply what I do."

In the intermediate draft of *PI* (1944–45; see *PU*: 692–93), this remark immediately precedes the one on forms of life. Seen in this light, a form of life is the bedrock where justifications end and following a rule in a certain way cannot be justified *except* by our following the rule in that way. Remark 242, on the other hand, does not follow §241 in either MS 124, 129, or the Intermediate version, signaling that Wittgenstein decided to put §§241 and 242 together only when he was preparing the final version of *PI*.

The rearrangement of the sequence of remarks that Wittgenstein made tells us something about the line of reasoning that he wanted to stimulate in the reader of the *Investigations*: from the absence of disputes on rule following among mathematicians to the question about human agreement and the clarification of agreement in definitions and in judgments, which is more broadly a clarification of the relationship between logic and its applications. At the same time, the examination of the early formulations and the early sequences allows us to follow Wittgenstein's own train of thought when he was ruminating on these ideas: the reflection originated from the example of continuing a series, in which the difficulty seems to be the explanation of the gap between one step and the following step, and the initial answer (which Wittgenstein rejects) appeals to either interpretation or intuition. When Wittgenstein formulated these ideas, the acknowledgment of the absence of doubt when one follows a rule – the acknowledgment of reasons giving out at a certain point (*PI* §211–13) – is what prompts the introduction of the notion of forms of life in this context. Agreement in forms of life is where one's spade strikes bedrock (*PI* §217). Later, in the final version of the *Investigations*, the remarks from *PI* §§210–13 (continuing a series) to *PI* §241 (agreement in forms of life) guide the reader, at a slower pace, we might say, from the issue of rule following to the notion of forms of life, passing through the acknowledgment of the absence of disputes in well-established practices such as mathematics.

The connection between the application of the rule and forms of life is indeed already present in Wittgenstein's writings in 1938, as is the distinction between agreement in opinions and agreement in forms of life. This remark is from MS 160, dated 1938, and it already includes a version of part of *PI* §241:

> "How is the application of a rule fixed?" – Do you mean, "logically" fixed? Either through other rules, or nothing at all. – Or do you mean: how is it, that we all apply it in agreement [*übereinstimmend*] in this way and not other-wise? By training, discipline, and the forms of our life [*die Formen unsres Lebens*]. It is not a consent [*Consens*] of opinion, but of forms of life [*Lebensformen*]. (MS 160: 26r–26v)

In the reflections that follow these lines, Wittgenstein discusses how "training, discipline, and the forms of our life" relate to logic. He claims that by emphasizing that there might be cases in which, for instance, the law of the excluded middle does not apply, or by observing that one should not be startled by a contradiction, he is not making an empirical point. He is not warning against assuming, *as a matter of empirical belief*, that the principle of the excluded middle is always true; rather, he is exhorting, "Get used to a variety of techniques" in order to see how thinking works. He is not treating logic as a matter of fact and logical principles as propositions that can be true or false. He is not claiming that the principle of noncontradiction (for instance) is not always true. He explains, "I don't want to eliminate a prejudice of opinion [*Vorurteil der Meinung*], *but of technique*" (MS 160: 27r; my emphasis). Note that here, Wittgenstein is using the same kind of sentence that he uses in *PI* §241: he is concerned with agreement or with prejudice not *in opinions* but in something else. This parallelism suggests comparing forms of life (as he mentions in connection with agreement) and techniques (as he mentions in connection with prejudices). A form of life, in this sense, is a complex set of techniques used and transmitted by training, and it is at the level of techniques that human beings agree in that they learn, use, and teach the same practices of continuing a series, or of "doing the same." Techniques solidify in judgments (*Urteile*; cf. *PI* §242) that become "prejudices" (*Vorurteile*; cf. MS 160: 27r), habitual and deeply entrenched ways of thinking. That is why such agreement is not only in definitions but also in judgments, and that is why it does not amount to abolishing logic, as *PI* §242 clarifies. Rather, it amounts to acknowledging the interconnectedness between logic itself and forms of life: logic is grounded in our learning, practicing, and teaching to follow rules in the way in which we follow rules. Logic in this sense, the way we practice logic, is part of our natural history (cf. Kuusela 2022: 50–55); again, this does not abolish logic but only makes it more explicit that an agreement in forms of life is a *presupposition* of logic itself (cf. *RFM*: 352–53, 430–31).

The topic of agreement in techniques is particularly relevant in *RFM*. Measuring and counting, Wittgenstein observes, are "use and custom among us" (*RFM*: 61), and agreement, or consensus, on calculating and on the results of calculations belongs to the "essence" of calculation (*RFM*: 193), where counting and calculating are important parts of our life (*RFM*: 37, 390). Several passages in this collection of remarks are helpful in shedding more light on forms of life, including one in which this notion is explicitly mentioned. To understand whether a pupil "possesses the rule inwardly" – that is, whether they are able to continue the series or "do the same" correctly in future occurrences – Wittgenstein observes, we normally look at how they react to a certain order; if they react the way we expect them to, we conclude that they "possess the rule inwardly." "But *this* is important," Wittgenstein adds, that this reaction, which is our guarantee of understanding, presupposes as a surrounding particular circumstances, particular forms of life and speech [*Lebens- und Sprachformen*]. (As there is no such thing as a facial expression without a face.)[26] (*RFM*: 414)

We understand whether someone is following a rule in the right way against the background of particular forms of life. There is nothing absolute in mathematics or logic, nothing abstracted and independent from the way we practice mathematics or draw logical inferences, but this does not mean that everything is arbitrary and changeable. Quite the opposite, these practices are "rigidly determined" (*RFM*: 409) and belong to an environment of activities without which we would not be able to recognize them as normal or correct, and perhaps not even as the expression of a rule (cf. *RFM*: 40). What counts as following a rule depends on the form of life in which it is embedded.

Wittgenstein's frequent use of imaginary examples of tribes with different mathematical practices, a seemingly bizarre logic, or an alien language, illustrates the same point, though from a different angle. He often asks his readers to imagine the circumstances under which they would be inclined to consider a certain practice of a foreign tribe as a case of (for instance) counting or measuring (*RFM*: 38, 96) or a certain word, gesture, or expression as having the same meaning as ours (*RFM*: 421) or a certain logic that, say, does not include negation or the law of contradiction as logic at all (*PI* §554). The most famous example is perhaps the tribe whose members pile timber in heaps of arbitrary height and then sell timber based on the area that it covers instead of the weight of wood or the number of logs (*RFM*: 94).[27] These cases of alien forms of logic and mathematics, where things become so far from our usual practices that we are uncertain whether to still call them logic or mathematics, have the effect of bringing logic and mathematics themselves back from a supposed supernatural realm to the forms of life in which they are embedded (*RFM*: 40). Mathematics and logic, Wittgenstein suggests, are not different from other areas of human experience where normativity (rule following) is involved. Questions similar to those about alien forms of counting or reasoning indeed can arise about alien forms of authority, the exercise and enforcement of power, social roles, obedience, and punishment (*RFM*: 352).

Forms of life, seen in this light, are the environment of agreement that is presupposed by the "hardness of the logical must" (*RFM*: 352–53), if there is such a thing, as well as by what we might call the "hardness of the social must." Another remark on forms of life, from MS 165 (tentatively dated 1941–4 by von

---

[26] Compare MS 124: 150, MS 127: 192, both probably from 1944.
[27] These examples stimulated a debate on the concept of "logical aliens"; more on this in Section 3.

Wright), makes a similar point regarding what counts as giving and following orders:

> Were we to arrive in a foreign country, with a foreign language and foreign customs, it could be easy in some cases to find a form of language and form of life [*Sprach- und Lebensform*] which we should define as giving orders and following orders; or maybe they would not possess a form of language and of life corresponding to our giving orders etc. And there may be a people which does not hold a form of life corresponding to our greeting. (MS 165: 110)[28]

Several remarks in published works have originated from this reflection. The best known is probably *PI* §206, where Wittgenstein answers the question about what we would be disposed to consider examples of giving and obeying orders and, more generally, about our interpretation of a foreign language by appealing to what is common among different human communities:

> Shared human behavior is the system of reference by means of which we interpret an unknown language. (*PI* §206)

The background against which we interpret another language, Wittgenstein states, is the "shared human behavior," or "the common behavior of mankind," in the previous translation made popular by Anscombe – a common behavior that shows some regularities in the use of words and in the connections between actions and words. It is at this level – the level of regular ways in which human beings follow rules – that human agreement takes place and defines the contours of language use.

To conclude regarding this aspect, Wittgenstein sometimes uses *Lebensformen* to direct our attention to the underlying deep agreement or consensus that characterizes and structures human beings' lives with rules and with words. Far from being merely conventional in the sense of stipulated or arbitrary (cf. Dummett 1959), such agreement is the framework that allows us to make sense of language games. At the same time, it is, to a certain extent, susceptible to change in response to changes in the ways in which we play such games. If there is something conventional in agreement, then that convention has the depth of very basic life practices and techniques that we cannot change at will, even if de facto they can undergo slow and usually imperceptible alterations through time.[29]

---

[28] Elsewhere, Wittgenstein provides other examples of alien countries or tribes with totally different customs that involve, for instance, always miming pain or never dissimulating anything (*Z* §§387–90, *LW II*: 27) or in which the natural laws themselves are different; for instance, colors constantly change or there is only one color (*RPP II* §§198–99).

[29] On Wittgenstein's notion of convention, see his own clarification in *WCL*: 234. See also Cavell 1962: 72, 1979: chapter 5; Gier 1980: 255; and Witherspoon 2003.

2.4 Cluster 3: The Given

The last cluster of remarks that I would like to consider focuses broadly on the notion of forms of life as "the given" that must be accepted, as Wittgenstein put it in *PPF*. All these remarks were written after the Second World War.

Let us start from the last two passages on forms of life in the *Investigations*, both of which belong to *PPF*. The first occurs at the very beginning of *PPF*:

> A dog believes his master is at the door. But can he also believe that his master will come the day after tomorrow? – And *what* can he not do here? – How do I do it? – What answer am I supposed to give to this?
>
> Can only those hope who can talk? Only those who have mastered the use of a language. That is to say, the manifestations of hope are modifications of this complicated form of life [*Lebensform*]. (If a concept points to a characteristic of human handwriting, it has no application to beings that do not write.) (*PPF* §1 [i 148])

This remark originates in MS 137 (115a [December 1948]), in which Wittgenstein does not actually use *Lebensform* but rather uses *Muster* and *Lebensmuster*, model or pattern of life (it becomes *Lebensform* in MS 144: 1 [1949]). The pattern of human life, Wittgenstein seems to suggest here, is one in which language plays an important role and shapes the manifestations of hope (as well as other feelings). The ways in which a human being shows and expresses hope include, for instance, the possibility of articulating it in *time* (it makes sense to say, "I hope she will arrive the day after tomorrow"). Although we say, "A dog believes his master is at the door," saying, "The dog hopes his master will arrive the day after tomorrow" makes little sense, not because the dog is incapable of certain feelings but because the way in which we describe hope in its temporal dimension is "at home" only for a form of life that includes the use of language. We can surely describe a dog that, for instance, having been left alone for a few days, feels sad and longs for his owners to return soon, but we would not use expressions such as "He hopes his owners will come back on Friday." This remark invites us to reflect on how the fabric of human life, with the characteristic ways in which we express and manifest feelings, is interwoven with language and how language has modified, articulated, and made complex the ways in which we experience and manifest a feeling such as hope.

An analogous reflection appears in *PI* §649, where it is applied to memory, and in *PI* §650, where it is applied to fear. Similarly, in *Z* §§518–20, Wittgenstein asks whether dogs can feel remorse and repent about something they did. Again, this feeling implies an articulated temporal dimension, and again Wittgenstein connects it to language ("Why can a dog feel fear but not remorse? Would it be right to say 'Because he can't talk'?"). However, the point, again, is not that as a matter of empirical possibility, an animal is not capable of this feeling. The point is that the way in which we describe this phenomenon, the concepts that we employ, are applicable in a fully meaningful way only to beings that possess a language.

The reflection about the interconnectedness of language, feelings, and the expression, recognition, and description of feelings that appears in *PPF*, therefore, is already present in some of Wittgenstein's earlier writings (though not *much* earlier); what is new in *PPF* §1 [i 148] is that Wittgenstein now uses the notion of *Lebenform* to clarify it. In this way, he also clarifies the very notion: at least on this occasion, it is a tool he is employing to highlight how certain phenomena and feelings that play a basic and important role in our life are inextricably connected with our speaking a language.[30]

The second remark on forms of life in *PPF*, and the last remark in the *Investigations*, introduces the theme of the given:

> What has to be accepted, the given, is – one might say – *forms of life [Lebensformen]*. (*PPF* §345 [xi 192])

In the preceding paragraphs in *PPF*, Wittgenstein is reflecting on the different ways in which we talk about certainty (and uncertainty): for instance, regarding other people's feelings or regarding mathematics. He observes that we sometimes talk of certainty (*Sicherheit*) as a sort of tonality of thought, but he invites us to think of it *not* as a feeling that arises in us when we are certain about something but rather as something that is manifested in people's actions. He observes that we talk of "subjective" and "objective" certainty, and these two words, rather than denoting different (perhaps psychological) phenomena, point to different language games (*PPF* §§339–40 [xi 191–92]; these topics are also explored at length in *OC*). Focusing on mathematical certainty, as he did in *PI* §240, he notes that mathematicians do not *quarrel* over the results of calculations because even if a dispute arises, it can be decided with certainty (*PPF* §§341–42 [xi 192]). What does this certainty depend on? Not on the reliability of ink and paper, although it is true that if ink and paper mysteriously and unpredictably altered, we could not calculate with them (we would have other means of calculation). Thus, where does the chain stop? "The given," what must be accepted, Wittgenstein says here, is forms of life. The complete agreement

---

[30] In MS 136: 140b–141b, the same line of reasoning applies to doubt: only in a life with language can doubt occur "so to speak in full bloom" (*in voller Blüte*) as "a variation of the forms of life [*Formen des Lebens*] of communication, question, and the like." Here, *Formen des Lebens* seems to refer to specific language games.

(*volle Übereinstimmung*) of mathematics is in the techniques of calculation that we use, teach, and learn (*PPF* §347 [xi 192]).

The remark on the given has given rise to interpretive disputes among Wittgensteinian commentators, sometimes being taken as the expression of a certain kind of conservatism and/or relativism because, if read out of context, it seems to assert that forms of life, however they are, must be accepted as they are. However, the point has more to do with the questionable *philosophical* notion of the given than with an alleged appeal to accept forms of life as they are. Examining the early formulation of this remark helps us see the point more clearly.

Interestingly, while the paragraphs that precede and follow *PPF* §345 [xi 192] have their origins in MS 138 (1949), Wittgenstein pulls *PPF* §345 [xi 192] from a former manuscript, MS 133, dating back to 1946–47. The lines that we find here were published in *RPP I* §630:

> Instead of the unanalysable, specific, indefinable: the fact that we act in such-and-such ways, e.g. *punish* certain actions, *establish* the state of affair thus and so, *give* orders, render accounts, describe colours, take an interest in others' feelings. What has to be accepted, the given – it might be said – are facts of living.

In the manuscript, what must be accepted is "*Lebensformen / Tatsachen des Lebens*," forms of life / facts of life (MS 133: 28v). When Wittgenstein places the final line of this remark in his MS 144 (the manuscript of *PPF*; see p. 102), he chooses to use "forms of life" instead of "facts of living." Note that in this remark, *actions* are emphasized (indeed, these words are underlined in the manuscript; see also *PPF* §339 [xi 191]).

What this early formulation clarifies is that Wittgenstein's mention of "the given" is to be read in connection with "the unanalyzable, specific, indefinable." The given, Wittgenstein is saying, the hard datum that philosophical analysis (including the kind of analysis that he himself proposed in the *Tractatus*) is seeking, must *not* be identified with a mysterious primum that is "specific" and cannot be analyzed or broken into smaller parts. Rather, a philosophical clarification of what is "given" and "specific" should point to what we do, to the basic facts of human life such as giving orders, following rules, punishing those who do not follow them, making reports, being interested in others' feelings, and describing colors (note the similarity between this list and the examples of language games in *PI* §23). In the context of *RPP I* §630, what stimulates this line of reasoning is the quite common idea that there is something specific in our experience of a certain color: something incommunicable that belongs only to the perceiver.

In relation to this, Wittgenstein observes that when we look at something red, we do not see something "specific" but rather "the *phenomena* that we *limit* by means of the language-game with the word 'red'" (*RPP I* §619). If we focus on such phenomena, we also realize that there is nothing mysterious and incommunicable in the experience of colors. We do communicate about colors: we agree on what is darker or lighter, and we match colors and compare them. Rather than wondering about the "specific" in the experience of colors, we should examine and describe what we do with colors (*RPP I* §621). These are the two remarks that come immediately before *RPP I* §630:

> "Colours are something specific. Not to be explained by anything else." How is this instrument used? – Describe the game with colours. The naming of colours, the comparison of colours, the production of colours, the connexion between colour and light and illumination, the connexion of colour with the eye, of notes with the ear, and innumerable other things. Won't what is "specific" about colours come out in this? How does one shew someone a colour; and how a note?
>
> When we talk to ourselves in thought: "Something happens; that's for sure." But the usefulness of these words is in reality just as unclear as that of the special psychological propositions that we are trying to explain.
>
> (*RPP I* §§628–29)

The exhortation to acknowledge that "the given" is nothing but forms of life, then, has its origins in this rebuttal of the alleged primitivity of a specific sensation or a specific feeling connected with the perception of colors or other psychological phenomena (a rebuttal of qualia, we might say).

Further evidence in favor of this interpretation comes from *PGL*, which collects students' notes on Wittgenstein's lectures on philosophical psychology. The remark on the given in MS 133 is from November 7, 1946. The following day, Wittgenstein started his class by observing, "We are trying to get at what we mean by 'specific', that is what we have in mind when we say, for instance, 'Thinking is a specific, simple property', or 'Red is specific'" (*PGL*: 261).[31] In these cases, he observes,

> There's a temptation to say, "Colour experience, sound experience, hoping, fearing, thinking, are specific" – as if you could define by concentration – but you can't. The specific is something that has to be *shown* publicly. What *can* be shown publicly and are specific are certain phenomena of life. . . . Take any

---

[31] The same lecture is reported at pp. 22 ff., 139 ff., and 261 ff. I am selecting from different reports here. Wittgenstein's target in much of *PGL* was probably William James (see Boncompagni 2019).

such phenomenon as comparing colours, measuring time, comparing lengths, playing games. These are specific. "I'll show you a thing we humans do"

(*PGL*: 23–24)

". . . an activity we humans do." (*PGL*: 264)

Seen in this framework, the remark on forms of life as the given assumes a broader significance. Far from claiming that we need to accept forms of life as they are, far from constituting a manifestation of either conservatism or relativism, this remark is rather the expression of Wittgenstein's wish to do away with appeals to the "specific" as the ultimate given that philosophy finds or postulates at the foundation of its analyses. The reference to forms of life instead is an antidote to this temptation, an antidote that reminds us of the practices and techniques that characterize our life and that a philosophical analysis cannot break down, factorize, or explain away.[32]

How does Wittgenstein characterize such a "given" in his later thought?

In the notes of *OC*, he talks of a form of life in terms of an "animal" certainty that is beyond justification. When one says, "I know," referring to obvious aspects of the world (for instance, "I know that that's a tree" when in front of a tree), if this "I know" makes any sense, he observes, it is as the expression of a sort of "*comfortable* certainty [*Sicherheit*]" (*OC* §357), an unquestioned sureness that, if questioned, would result in bewilderment; one wouldn't even understand what a doubt would look like in such a matter. He continues,

> Now I would like to regard this certainty, not as something akin to hastiness or superficiality, but as a form of life [*Lebensform*]. (That is very badly expressed and probably badly thought as well.)
>
> But that means I want to conceive it as something that lies beyond being justified or unjustified; as it were, as something animal.[33]
>
> (*OC* §§358–59, from MS 175: 55v–56r)

It is not a matter of hastiness that when we walk down a familiar road, we are confident that the ground will not collapse under our feet; it is not because we are superficial or lazy that before stepping out our front door, we do not check to see whether a ravine has opened during the night. Note that both things *could* happen; we are not able to absolutely rule out the extremely unlikely hypotheses that someone put a hidden trap in our pathway or that a ravine opened during the night without waking us up. However, we act with confident certainty that

---

[32] On forms of life as the given, see also Boncompagni 2016b.

[33] Compare *RFM*: 253: "We do not accept e.g. a multiplication not yielding the same result everytime. And what we expect with certainty is essential to our whole life."

things are as we expect them to be. This form of sureness can be described as "something animal" (although this is "badly thought"), arguably because it is the same kind of sureness with which an animal acts in its environment, a sureness that shows in action.[34] In the human form of life, this sureness also shows in our ordinary comfortable and confident use of familiar words and not doubting their meaning when we use them. In this sense, "the absence of doubt belongs to the essence of the language-game" (*OC* §370), and the sureness of "I know this is a hand" shows in our mastering statements such as "I feel pain in this hand" or "I once broke this hand." It is part of these language games that the existence of my hand is not put in doubt (*OC* §371).

Wittgenstein's treatment of "I know" here coheres with his treatment of "the specific" in the remarks just examined. "I know" does not express a special feeling attached to our belief that marks it as a certainty; rather, if there is something specific and "given" that is expressed by "I know," it is the unquestioned sureness shown in our actions and in our language games. Such a sureness characterizes our most basic and common practices, and in this sense, it is a dimension that is shared by all human beings (*PI* §206). There is something *instinctive* in it (cf. *Z* §391, *OC* §475): it manifests in the naturalness of our behavior.

Interestingly, in an unpublished remark, Wittgenstein seems even to equate form of life with an instinctive movement. In a reflection on the origins of the "game" of pretending, he pictures a young child crying. When faced with a crying child, nobody would speak of pretending, he observes. At this stage, he adds, "if something looks like pretending it would be an animal kind of pretense, a form of life [*Lebensform*] // [variant: an instinctive movement]." It is only after the child has started mastering certain courses of action or routines that we can recognize something similar to pretense in their behavior (MS 137: 59a [1948]).[35]

Note that the instinctiveness of "animal certainty" is not in contradiction with the human form of life being essentially linguistic. On the contrary, talking of our form of life as a sort of animal certainty highlights how fundamental linguistic competence and behavior are for us (as is well known, McDowell [1994] talked of second nature in this respect). Interwoven with the linguistic dimension is the normativity of the human form of life; in fact, Wittgenstein's examples, as we saw, are often focused on following rules, giving orders, obeying or disobeying, punishing, and rewarding. Talking of form of life in this respect, then, amounts to pointing to how speaking a language and

---

[34] The connection between certainty and action is explored at length in Moyal-Sharrock's (2004) study.

[35] Translation from Schulte 2010: 131. For an interpretation, see Hacker 2015: 12.

following rules are part of the "animality" of human beings, part of what makes our form of (for example) hope different from a dog's hope. Speaking a language and following rules are "things we humans do," and this is the given at which the analysis must stop, without attempting to go further and seek more elementary units of analysis.

Another remark on forms of life, the last one we are considering, was written only one month after *OC* §§358–59 and points to another feature of the human form of life, which Wittgenstein calls "imponderable evidence."

This passage belongs to a set of reflections in which Wittgenstein is dealing with our practices of understanding (and sometimes not understanding) others. Our understanding and perception of other people's feelings, emotions, and thoughts, Wittgenstein observes, rest on a peculiar kind of evidence that is "imponderable": it cannot be pondered, weighed, or measured because it is qualitative rather than quantitative.[36] By observing their facial expressions and bodily movements, we can know with immediate certainty that a friend is (for instance) sad, angry, or disappointed, although we would not be able to fully explain in words what makes us so certain. We do not have a standard against which we measure the width of a smile in order to understand how much happiness it expresses. We just see our friend's state of mind in their face or in a gesture, sometimes even when they try to hide it from us. We can also, of course, be wrong: our friend might be able to truly dissimulate their disappointment, sadness, or happiness. This sort of expert, although fallible, knowledge of human beings (*Menschenkenntnis*; see *PPF* §355 [xi 193]), with its interplay of certainty and uncertainty, is an important feature of our life with others. It is a capacity that we learn and teach, that we employ daily, and that some people possess to a greater degree than others.

The section of MS 176 in which Wittgenstein mentions forms of life in connection with imponderable evidence was not published in *OC*, as were the preceding and following sections (pages 22–81 according to von Wright 1993: 509); instead, it found its way to volume II of *LPP*, which ends with these lines:

> And now the question remains whether we would give up our language-game which rests on "imponderable evidence" and frequently leads to uncertainty, if it were possible to exchange it for a more exact one which by and large would have similar consequences. For instance, we could work with a mechanical "lie detector" and redefine a lie as that which causes a deflection on the lie detector.

---

[36] Imponderable evidence also characterizes aesthetic understanding and judgment. See Boncompagni 2018.

> So the question is: Would we change our way of living [*Lebensform*] if this or that were provided for us? – And how could I answer that? (*LWP II*: 95, from MS 176: 51v; see also *LW I* §§ 917–38)

The theme of dissimulation, the imaginary case of a tribe where no one dissimulates, and the hypothesis of the lie detector also appear in other writings (see, for instance, *LW II*: 27 and *RFM*: 212), but here, Wittgenstein connects them to the notion of forms of life. The question asked in this remark – whether we would change our form of life if something such as a lie detector were provided – remains unanswered, and obviously so ("How could I answer that?"). A form of life without imponderable evidence is something we can hardly make sense of because the practices of imponderable evidence are too deeply ingrained in the patterns of our life.

We might be tempted to ask and possibly answer the question about the lie detector as if it were an empirical matter, a hypothesis that ideally could be scientifically tested. What would happen to us if a portable, 100 percent error-free lie detector were invented, everyone constantly had one with them, and a lie were redefined as a statement that made the lie detector beep? However, Wittgenstein's question is not of this nature. In my view, his question is a rhetorical device that invites us to work at a conceptual level: to explore the boundaries of our concepts, that is, the boundaries of our practices with words. Trying to imagine our form of life without the phenomena of imponderable evidence is akin to trying to imagine different facts of nature that might give rise to different concepts (*PPF* §366 [xii 195]). Although the alternative concepts themselves are hardly imaginable, what the attempts succeed in bringing to our attention is *the connection* between facts of nature and our conceptual repertoire (Hertzberg 2011). Similarly, although we would hardly be able to imagine an alien form of life in which the automatic lie detector is a substitute for imponderable evidence, what the question succeeds in bringing to our attention is *the interwovenness* of our form of life and our concepts – what we are disposed to call a human being, for instance, or the way in which we employ words to express and describe emotions and thoughts.

Taking this question as empirical, that is, taking the very connection between facts of nature and concepts as the object of an empirical investigation, leads to a naturalistic interpretation of Wittgenstein's notion of forms of life. However, Wittgenstein's constant insistence on the distinction between an empirical and a conceptual investigation should caution us against this kind of outcome. The remarks on forms of life as "the given," seen in this light, are ultimately an attempt to nullify this temptation.[37]

---

[37] I expand on this in Section 4.

3 Interpretations of Forms of Life

3.1 Overview

Making some order of the vast and complicated literature on Wittgenstein's notion of forms of life is a difficult task, and a complete survey, given the number of voices at play, is simply impossible. It would not be useful in any case; it would be more confusing than clarifying. What is possible and possibly clarifying is identifying the main ideas and trends that shaped the debate over the years. This is what I am doing in the present section, opening with an examination of some early interpretations of forms of life (among which are those offered by J. F. M. Hunter, Stanley Cavell, Nicholas Gier, Baker and Hacker, and Jonathan Lear) and then adding some later voices, not with the presumption of being exhaustive but with the aim of pointing out the most relevant points of controversy among commentators. This also allows us to briefly consider some wider discussions related to forms of life, such as those of relativism and conservatism, the nature of rules, and naturalism.

Last, in the concluding section of this essay, I compare the map of interpretations with the analysis of Wittgenstein's own remarks provided in Section 2 in order to determine what these readings capture and perhaps what is left out. As will emerge, while some sort of support can be found for all interpretations in *some* of Wittgenstein's remarks, none of the interpretations makes sense of all of the remarks. However, such a result lends support to a methodological reading of this notion, as opposed to a substantive one.

3.2 Some Classical Interpretations

One of the first articles to systematically deal with forms of life is Hunter (1968). After listing the five occurrences of *Lebensform* and *Lebensformen* in the *Investigations*, Hunter illustrates four possible interpretations of this notion:

1. A form of life is a language game, more specifically, a formalized, standardized, and shared language game.
2. A form of life is "a sort of package of mutually related tendencies to behave in various ways," a set of natural behaviors (smiling, frowning, etc.) that "we are jointly inclined to engage in" and that is standardly connected with certain language games.
3. A form of life is a way of life, or a style, a fashion, something that has to do with the values, the culture, and the socioeconomic structure of a society.
4. A form of life is something typical of a living being, similar to growing, eating, walking, and reacting in a certain way to the environment.

The last of these interpretations is the one that Hunter favors, labeling it "the organic account" and explaining that it does not rule out but rather encompasses complex and cultural behaviors, such as the speaking of a language. In this view, constructing appropriate sentences and expressing oneself are complex and natural operations that a human being learns to do, similar to walking or dancing. This allows Wittgenstein – in Hunter's view – to account for language use without appealing to private mental acts, a constant polemical target for him. Hunter's "organic account" therefore considers form of life a biological feature of every human being rather than a social phenomenon; in this view, using the right words during a linguistic exchange ultimately amounts to a sort of blind reaction to a given situation because this use of words has been built into us: it is part of our organic functioning.

Hunter's article is a good starting point because it is already possible to identify here some of the questions that many interpreters struggled with: Is a form of life a social/cultural phenomenon, or is it a feature that belongs to the individual as an organism? Is there one single human form of life, or is there a plurality of forms of life, connected perhaps with the plurality of language games or with the plurality of cultural contexts in which human beings live?

One of the few authors that Hunter cites in his seminal piece is Stanley Cavell, specifically his article "The Availability of Wittgenstein's Later Philosophy," first published in 1962. In it, Cavell describes the learning of a language and our capacity to project the use of words from one context to another as

> a matter of our sharing routes of interest and feeling, modes of response, senses of humor and of significance and of fulfillment, of what is outrageous, of what is similar to what else, what a rebuke, what forgiveness, of when an utterance is an assertion, when an appeal, when an explanation – all the whirl of organism Wittgenstein calls "forms of life." (Cavell 1962: 74)

Cavell, like Hunter, stresses the relevance of the "organic" element in forms of life, that is, naturality. As emerges perhaps with more clarity in slightly later writings, he does so in order to counterbalance the tendency to speak of forms of life in exclusively sociocultural terms (which corresponds to Hunter's third reading). However, he does not *deny* the relevance of the sociocultural aspect: he just maintains that it is sometimes overemphasized. In other words, Cavell acknowledges two dimensions of forms of life: the "horizontal," or anthropological, dimension connected with the social and cultural traits of a society or a group and with the social nature of language; and the "vertical," or biological, dimension, where the focus is on our "real needs" as human beings (cf. *PI* §108), something we risk losing contact with in philosophy and that Wittgenstein instead (and Cavell after him) aims to rescue (Cavell 1988, 2004a, 2004b).

In response to Hunter, Gier (1980) opposes the organic account and favors a sociocultural reading, claiming that Wittgenstein's idea of human life cannot be reduced to the biological level; in fact, human life is qualitatively different from animal life, and such a qualitative difference cannot be reduced (as Hunter does, in Gier's view) to an empirical one. Based on Wittgenstein's acceptance of the translation of *Lebensformen* as "ways of life,"[38] as well as on the relevance of Spranger's notion of forms of life for Wittgenstein, Gier concludes that the sociocultural aspects of human forms of life must be prominent in the interpretation. While acknowledging that the organic and the cultural account need not be in contradiction, Gier (1980: 255) insists that the former does not capture "the wholeness of the speaking situation": biology is a necessary but not sufficient condition for forms of life.

The same point is made by Baker and Hacker in volume II of their commentary on *PI* (2009, first published in 1985): they oppose organic interpretations, claiming that they are based on a reading of the Wittgensteinian remarks taken out of context. Indeed, in their view, some aspects of forms of life are "biologically natural," but others are "culturally natural," or "natural for us" after a certain training. Therefore, the idea that certain conceptual structures are necessary for us *because of our nature* is mistaken (Baker and Hacker 2009: 220).[39] The idea of "natural history" that Wittgenstein advocates is, in their view, predominantly anthropological, not biological. "In short – they conclude – the natural history of man is a history of a convention-forming, rule-following, concept-exercising, language-using animal – a cultural animal" (2009: 221; also in the 1984 edition: 241), and the concept of forms of life is not primarily biological but cultural. Hacker (2015) further stresses the point, although he also argues that the notion of forms of life itself is actually not particularly relevant, as it is a "surface ornament" of Wittgenstein's real point, namely, the proposal of an ethnological conception of language (2015: 18).

In contrast to Baker and Hacker, however, Gier goes beyond a sociocultural view and proposes a complex account of forms of life articulated in four levels:

> (1) a biological level from which (2) unique human activities like pretending, grieving, etc. are then expressed in (3) various cultural styles that in turn have their formal ground in (4) a general socio-linguistic framework (Wittgenstein's *Weltbild*). (Gier 1980: 245)

What Gier wants to avoid in rejecting the organic view is a sort of metaphysics of natural facts, and what he wants to suggest is that when Wittgenstein speaks of "natural history" (for instance, *Z* §469, *RPP I* §§46, 78), a notion that

---

[38] As we have seen in Section 2, the translation he accepted was actually "way of living."

[39] The latter straightforward claim is only in the 2009 revised edition.

Gier considers equivalent to forms of life, he does so in opposition to natural *science*. Natural history is not an empirical science, and Wittgenstein's notion of *Lebensformen* is not an attempt to explain the relationship between nature and culture, for instance, in terms of physiology and psychology. Gier's solution points in a completely different direction: *Lebensformen* are "the formal conditions, the patterns in the weave of our lives, that make a meaningful world possible, . . . existential equivalents of Kant's *Bedingungen der Möglichkeit der Erfahrung*": they play a *transcendental function* (Gier 1980: 257).

Gier was neither the first nor the only proponent of a transcendental reading of forms of life. According to Bernard Williams (1974), the notion of form of life represents a sort of "pluralization" of the transcendental subject that Wittgenstein presents in the *Tractatus*. While in the *Tractatus*, Wittgenstein affirms that "the limits of my language mean the limits of my world" (*T* 5.6), in later works, he suggests that "the limits of our language mean the limits of our world" (Williams 1974: 82), where the "our" refers to a transcendental "we" captured by the notion of *Lebensform*. Without claiming that Wittgenstein explicitly puts forth a transcendental account of forms of life, Williams argues that this view, perhaps implicit or incomplete, can be traced in his later writings. Acknowledging that some passages in Wittgenstein seem to tell a different story, even a relativist one in some cases, William argues that such apparent incongruences can actually be explained and made sense of in a transcendental reading; indeed, when Wittgenstein imagines radically different and alien ways of living, he is actually exploring and inviting his readers to explore the limits of our own form of life, the transcendental possibilities and boundaries that *we* have.

Jonathan Lear's transcendental view of Wittgenstein develops in dialogue with Barry Stroud (see Lear 1984, Stroud 1984), as the two authors are in contrast for their interpretation not only of Wittgenstein but also of Kant (Stroud sees Kant as an idealist; Lear considers this a skeptical position and sees Kant instead as a constitutivist). Here, the analysis is limited to Wittgenstein. The aspect emphasized in Lear's reading is that "meaning is use" is only one part of Wittgenstein's view of meaning, the other being his emphasis on *understanding*. Wittgenstein indeed repeatedly investigates our capacity to grasp meaning "in a flash," and with this, in Lear's view, he aims to legitimize a sort of transcendental "I understand" that must accompany each of my representations.[40] In addition, in Wittgenstein's approach (in contrast to Kant's), language has a fundamental role. According to Lear, if language is to be recognized as

---

[40] It can be argued, however, that Wittgenstein criticizes, rather than espouses, the tendency to talk of "grasping meaning in a flash" or "at a stroke"; see, for instance, *PI* §§191, 197. More on this in Section 3.

a means of communication, not only does the "I understand" need to be acknowledged but also a "we are so minded" should accompany each of our representations, where "being so minded" amounts to sharing "perceptions of salience, routes of interest, feelings of naturalness in following a rule that constitute being part of a form of life" (Lear 1984, 229; the passage echoes Cavell 1962: 74). Therefore, if on the one hand, a form of life is something we can describe, on the other hand, it is what makes language and description possible, and these two aspects – the empirical and the transcendental, we might say – are what Wittgenstein attempts to keep together in a sort of "transcendental anthropology."[41]

Another point already highlighted by Hunter and widely debated afterward is whether for Wittgenstein, there is a singular human form of life or several different forms of life. An early commentator who is inclined to the latter view (that there are several forms of life connected with several language games) is Max Black (1978), who claims that "form of life" applies to the activity or set of activities that are necessary to produce meaningful utterances in a given language game and that a language game is part of a form of life. A pluralist view is also advanced by Glock (1996), who claims that a form of life is a culture or a social formation, that is, all the collective activities in which language games are embedded. On these grounds, Glock opposes the transcendental view, claiming that the aim of the notion of a form of life is precisely to detranscendentalize the contrast between grammar and matters of fact by showing that grammar is an integral part of our practices.

While Glock claims that there are different forms of life, Newton Garver (1984, 1994) argues that there is just one human form of life, and different language games belong to it. Like Gier, Garver emphasizes the relevance of natural history as opposed to natural science, and like Lear and Williams, he sees something transcendental in the notion of form of life; in his view, Wittgenstein identifies in some features of our natural world transcendental elements that constitute unquestionable "primitives" for us. In this sense, our form of life (the one and only human form of life) is the object of Wittgenstein's version of transcendental knowledge. When the plural is used, it refers to nonhuman (animal and imaginary) forms of life and not to different human cultures or styles or ways of living.

The transcendental readings as well as the idea that there is only one human form of life faced some criticism. Contra Williams, Malcolm (1982) claims that there is no point in comparing the early and late Wittgenstein because in the

---

[41] Another voice in the transcendentalist field is Rudder Baker 1984, who builds on both Williams and Lear.

latter, there are no signs of idealism or transcendentalism; moreover, when Wittgenstein uses the plural "we," he refers to definite groups of people existing (or imaginatively existing) in the world and not to an all-encompassing transcendental subject (262). Similarly, contra Garver, Haller (2014; originally published in 1988) claims that when Wittgenstein uses the plural, it is because he does refer to other human societies, real or imaginary, and even when he uses the singular (for instance, in *PI* §19, on imagining a language amounting to imagining a form of life), he clearly implies the existence of a plurality of forms of life. Haller goes so far as to claim that the existence of people who use scales and concepts of color different from ours (an example that Wittgenstein uses often, as we saw, and that is often thought of as an exercise in the limits of our concepts) is "an empirically well-established fact" (135). Haller's aim is to draw attention to an empirical inclination in Wittgenstein that in his perception is (was) overlooked in the debate. Baker and Hacker (2009: 221–23) also claim that Wittgenstein is not concerned with one human form of life but with a plurality of forms of life.

Finally, there are interpretations that highlight the existence of both dimensions: a multiplicity of human forms of life within the fundamental unity of one human form of life (for instance, Conway 1989, Moyal-Sharrock 2015). As will emerge soon, the methodological reading that I am defending also acknowledges the coexistence of both dimensions in Wittgenstein's work.

3.3 A Map of Positions

The interpretations of forms of life just examined highlight a set of themes that appear repeatedly. In this section, I identify the major axes around which the debate rotates, and on this basis, I propose a sort of conceptual map of the different positions that can be identified in the literature.[42] Some authors deal with only one or two of these axes, but identifying and disentangling the different dimensions at play is a useful exercise. In fact, attached to these dimensions are more general issues that are of interest not only for the niche of the Wittgensteinian literature but also for relevant and current debates in the philosophical community overall. After delineating the map, I will therefore hint at these wider debates and at how Wittgenstein has been used to support sometimes diametrically opposed visions.

Based on the sample of readings just examined, it seems to me that the relevant axes of discussion are the following.

---

[42] I am building here on my previous work (Boncompagni 2015) and combining it with Stern's (2004: 161).

3.3.1 Natural versus Cultural

Some authors claim that Wittgenstein's forms of life are biological or organic and that with this notion, he wanted to emphasize that human beings have certain features in virtue of their organisms being as they are. In this sense, talk of forms of life helps us see the "animality" of the human being, while at the same time, it helps us see what sets human beings apart from other nonhuman animals: chiefly, the speaking of a language and the development and articulation of a whole set of experiences, practices, and habits that language makes possible. The point of this reading is that what makes us human is as natural and organic as what makes a dog a dog or a fly a fly; therefore, what we normally denote as cultural and normative is itself natural, a part of our organism, we might say. Hunter is, of course, the exemplary case here, and so *in part* is Cavell – when he stresses the relevance of the vertical dimension of the notion of forms of life. On the other side of the axis are those authors who instead see in Wittgenstein's forms of life a description of the various broadly cultural features of our social life, including language, conventions, social norms, religion, and systems of ethics but also styles of life, fashion, social and economic structures, and art in its various manifestations. These authors – among whom are Baker and Hacker, the "horizontal" side of Cavell, and Glock – underline the continuity between Wittgenstein's idea of culture and his idea of forms of life, seeing in the latter a development, instead of a replacement, of the former. Both contenders can and in fact usually do acknowledge the relevance of the other aspect, but they generally do so by subsuming it under the aspect that they consider prevalent. For instance, Hunter claims that culture is an aspect of our nature, while Baker and Hacker claim that human nature is essentially cultural.

3.3.2 One versus Many

A second axis of debate concerns whether Wittgenstein talks of forms of life in the singular or in the plural. The debate is not so much on whether Wittgenstein uses *Lebensform* or *Lebensformen* (he evidently uses both) as on whether he means that there is only one form of life or a plurality of forms of life. For instance, according to *PI* §19, "to imagine a language means to imagine a form of life"; does this mean that there are different forms of life connected to different languages or that whenever one imagines a language, one imagines the human, linguistic form of life? While for *PI* §19, the former interpretation seems more plausible, in other cases, Wittgenstein's remarks suggest that the human form of life is one and the same; see, for instance, his example of hope being "a modification of this complicated form of life" (*PPF* §1 [xi 192]) and his reference to the common behavior of humankind (*PI* §206). Among the readings that we examined, Hunter and (especially) Garver tend to interpret form of life in the singular, while Black, Malcolm, and Haller emphasize Wittgenstein's insistence on plurality.

One might think that the organic versus cultural and singular versus plural debates overlap in the sense that those who claim that there is only one form of life are the same as those who claim that the form of life is organic, and those who claim that there is a plurality of forms of life are the same as those who claim that forms of life are cultural. While some overlap does in fact exist, this need not necessarily be the case, as the concepts at play clearly do not overlap. Therefore, it is totally plausible to claim that the (one and only) human form of life is essentially cultural and normative without relying on the organic constitution of human bodies. Conversely, it is also plausible – albeit debatable – to imagine different human forms of life based on differences in human organisms (controversial notions of race and gender might support this view).

3.3.3 Empirical versus Transcendental

Finally, a third debate in the literature on forms of life concerns whether Wittgenstein's point of view is empirical – having to do with the description of actual groups of individuals, societies, or cultures – or transcendental – having to do, broadly, with an account of the conditions of possibility of meaning and linguistic practices. According to the former, Wittgenstein's attitude is essentially descriptive, and "forms of life" is the term he uses to capture the empirically ascertainable interconnectedness between what human beings do and the sphere of meaning and language. This does not necessarily flatten a philosophical reflection into a scientific one, based on observation, quantification, experiments and verification; rather, according to several proponents of this view, Wittgenstein's approach is essentially anthropological, and the forms of investigation and understanding that he seeks are based on interpretive and qualitative rather than quantitative methods. Examples of empirical readings are those offered by Haller and Malcolm. On the other side of the spectrum are commentators who instead point out that an investigation of forms of life *cannot* have an empirical nature because forms of life are conditions of the possibility of meaning, intelligibility, and language. This is the transcendental reading of forms of life, according to which Wittgenstein's remarks are not meant as descriptions of actual activities and communities but rather as an exploration of 'the limits of our world" or of the framework that allows for meaning itself. As we saw, classical examples of these positions, which ideally connect Wittgenstein to the Kantian tradition, are presented by Williams and Lear.

Generally, readings that oppose the transcendental view are more likely to be pluralistic, and, as mentioned, most pluralistic readings espouse a cultural view. However, again, this need not necessarily be the case. One might argue, for instance, in favor of a transcendental view grounded in the human organic nature as well as in our cultural framework (or in different cultural frameworks).

3.4 Wider Debates

3.4.1 Cultural Relativism and Conservatism

One issue that is often mentioned in connection with Wittgenstein's notion of forms of life is cultural relativism. Needless to say, it is not my concern here to explore this huge debate in depth, but it is interesting to see how different approaches to forms of life play out in the discussion.

The topic of relativism typically emerges in interpretations that embrace a pluralist and empirical view of forms of life. This is the case, for instance, of Glock (1996: 126), according to whom Wittgenstein endorses a form of *cultural* relativism resulting from the *conceptual* relativism of his idea of the autonomy of language. Emmett (1990) also espouses a pluralist and empirical view against transcendental interpretations and shows a sympathetic attitude toward relativism. However, relativism usually also elicits a worry related to the intelligibility and alleged incommensurability of different forms of life. To remain in an empirical and pluralist approach: if another culture or society is intelligible only by virtue of a shared form of life, then in the absence of a shared form of life, that other culture or society remains unintelligible and ultimately inaccessible. A corollary is the alleged impossibility of criticizing different forms of life, given that the parameters and categories for criticism cannot but be internal to a form of life itself.

Such worries can also arise from a transcendental position according to which a form of life is the framework that provides the conditions of possibility for a language or culture. This approach exacerbates the problem of the accessibility or even the conceivability of alien forms of life because it entails that one's (transcendental) form of life, while enabling one to understand and live one's own culture, by the same token precludes one from alien conceptual possibilities. When Williams reflects on what he calls, pluralizing the early Wittgenstein, "the limits of our language," and when Lear reflects on what he calls "the disappearance of the 'we,'" the problem they are confronting is precisely this. The "we" in "we are so minded" disappears because in our world, being minded just *is* being minded as we are. How, then, can we access another way of being minded? Is this conceivable?

One of the most important names that comes to mind when speaking of relativism in connection with Wittgenstein is Peter Winch. Usually considered an exponent of relativism, Winch (1990: 100) famously claims that "criteria of logic are not a direct gift of God, but arise out of, and are only intelligible in the context of, ways of living or modes of social life." The example he provides is that of science and religion, taken as two different forms of life: science and religion have their own criteria of logic (where logic is intended in a broad sense); therefore, the criteria of religion are not intelligible in the framework of science, and vice versa. The criteria themselves are not assessable in an objective, independent way: as such, they are neither logical not illogical, neither rational nor irrational, because they define the standards of rationality itself. This seems to be a straightforward statement of relativism and incommensurability. However, on other occasions, Winch also argues that some presuppositions are common to any community, such as truthfulness (a moral condition of language, in his view) and integrity (a moral condition for any social role and human institution) (Winch 1959–60). When concerned with the intelligibility of other cultures, Winch also emphasizes the existence of "deep objects of human concerns," such as (following Giambattista Vico) birth, death, and sexual relations; these "limiting notions" provide a common ground from which understanding another form of life becomes feasible (Winch 1964: 317–18). For understanding to be possible, one must appeal to these deep common concerns, to what is most basic in human beings, so that one can glimpse what *makes sense*, what has importance, in another's form of life; this requires the enlargement of one's criteria of intelligibility and one's standards and possibly even a shift in one's own way of life.

Wittgenstein, as we saw in the previous section, often provides examples that seem to be at the limits of intelligibility, challenging our imaginative abilities and demanding reflection on what we are disposed to accept as variations in our familiar concepts and habits of thought. His imaginary tribes, as in the famous case of the wood sellers, are indeed interpreted sometimes as proving and sometimes as refuting the idea that radically alien forms of life are intelligible. Stroud (1965) considers these examples only apparently intelligible. He claims that while at first sight, we seem to be able to understand them (after all, we talk about them), when we look at them more closely and try to trace their implications – try to imagine ourselves selling wood the way that tribe does, and what it would mean for other portions of our life – their intelligibility drastically diminishes, and we find ourselves at a loss. This is not, however, because these examples violate logical necessity. Our troubles in understanding them are compatible with the acknowledgment of the contingency of our own rules, and this is, in Stroud's view, the point Wittgenstein is making: the experiments are meant to show the contingency of our ways of calculating, measuring, reasoning, and ultimately living – where contingency is not to be confused with arbitrariness or mere convention. On the other hand, Canfield (1975) and more recently Medina (2003) claim that Wittgenstein's examples *are* intelligible, and the point that Wittgenstein makes with his creative science-fiction anthropology is precisely that we *are* able to understand and make room for radically alternative systems of reasoning. This position may be more akin to a form of contextualism than to relativism.

Winch's appeal to the deepest concerns of human beings obviously resonates with Wittgenstein's appeal to the "common behavior of mankind" as the system of reference through which we interpret an unknown language. Glock's version of cultural relativism, indeed, does not preclude the possibility of understanding another form of life, provided that it shares with ours "common perceptual capacities, needs, and emotions" (1996: 128).[43] Relatedly, for Moyal-Sharrock (2015, 2017), Wittgenstein's naturalism on the human form of life provides a stopping place for relativism. In her view, indeed, Wittgenstein can be considered a relativist only in the sense that he denies the existence of absolute truths about the world but does not endorse other claims that are sometimes associated with relativism, for example, that there is no objective, universal basis for knowledge and that any theory is as good as another (Moyal-Sharrock 2017: 223–24).[44]

A related worry that is usually associated with relativism and the incommensurability of forms of life is, indeed, the impossibility of rational critique. If a form of life sets its own standards of rationality, it is argued, then every possible justification is internal to it, and while criticism and reform remain possible within a form of life, criticizing a form of life from the outside cannot be a matter of rational argumentation (which presupposes some standards of rationality) but is, at best, a matter of persuasion (Glock 1996: 126; cf. *OC* §§261, 612). The charge of not allowing for rational critique has often been raised against Wittgenstein. Leaving aside some notoriously controversial (mis) readings, such as those of Ernst Gellner (who described Wittgenstein's perspective as "cultural-communal mysticism" and depicted him as a conservative defender of the *Gemeinschaft* [Gellner 1998: 75]) and Herbert Marcuse

---

[43] What remains precluded in Glock's view is only the intelligibility of nonhuman forms of life, whether animal forms of life or imaginary aliens (Glock 1996: 128). Glock indeed argues that this is what Wittgenstein was suggesting when he observed, "If a lion could talk, we wouldn't be able to understand it" (*PPF* §327 [xi 190]): if a lion had a sort of feline language, it would not be intelligible to us because the lion's form of life and behavioral repertoire would be too alien to us. (One might wonder, however, whether all living sentient beings share some even more basic features, such as the need to eat, survival instinct, and pain behavior.)

[44] On Wittgenstein and relativism, see also Coliva 2010; Kusch 2013, 2021.

(who harshly criticized Wittgenstein's alleged quietism, describing it as sado-masochistic and self-humiliating [Marcuse 1991: 178]), the *j'accuse* generally derives from combining a relativist outlook on the notion of forms of life with an emphasis on Wittgenstein's quietism, interpreted as the idea that philosophy can only describe phenomena and cannot attempt to either explain or change them. Here is an example:

> All criticism presupposes a form of life, a language, that is, a tradition of agreements; every judgment is necessarily embedded in traditions. That is why traditions cannot be judged. "One can only describe here" Wittgenstein wrote in 1931 "and say: this is what human life looks life". . . . All the time Wittgenstein strives to show that the given form of life is the ultimate givenness, that the given form of life cannot be consciously transcended. Wittgenstein is of course perfectly aware of the fact that there are different forms of life, different ultimate givennesses. And that these different forms of life all have the same value. . . . [I]t is an unalterable anthropological fact . . . that any human being must, in order to be a human being, be constrained by some form of life, by some network of tradition. (Nyíri 1981: 159)

What is apparent here is a common reading of the Wittgensteinian passage on forms of life as "the given" interpreted as an appeal to accept a form of life as it is, without attempting to criticize or change it. Relatedly, human beings are seen as "constrained" by a form of life and as obeying rules blindly in observance of the normative context in which they live. In this light, Wittgenstein's emphasis on description that must replace explanation (*PI* §109) is a plea for a "quiet" philosophy that must not challenge the status quo. However, as we saw in the previous section and as others have argued, the passage on the given is not intended in a political sense, and Wittgenstein's target there is not a philosophical project of social or political critique. The point he is making is about the methods and aims of philosophical analysis. Similarly, the appeal to description is set not against a philosophical project of critique but against philosophers' temptation to theorize about the ultimate causes of phenomena. In this light, "accepting" forms of life means acknowledging that the task of philosophy is to create awareness of the primacy and philosophical "unanalyz-ability" of our belonging to a form of life and of how only with reference to this can we make sense of language and meaning, which *is* compatible with the possibility of criticism both from within and from outside a form of life. In Putnam's words,

> Recognizing that there are certain places where one's spade is turned; recognizing, with Wittgenstein, that there are places where our explanations run out, isn't saying that any particular place is *permanently* fated to be 'bedrock', or that a particular belief is forever immune from criticism. . . . Our moral

images are in a process of development and reform. But it is to say that at each stage of that development and reform, there will be places, many places, at which we have to say: "This is where my spade is turned." None of this goes against the idea that rational criticism of a moral vision is possible. . . . This is *not* Feyerabendian relativism. It *is* a rejection of the project of Epistemology with a capital E. (Putnam 1987: 85)

In this view, the Wittgensteinian notion of forms of life inhabits a terrain that stands equally apart from both the "big" project of epistemology – one based on traditional notions of truth and objectivity – and the problematic implications of certain forms of relativism. Even though Wittgenstein might seem to be unconcerned with social critique in his own philosophy, an interpretation of his notion of forms of life as banishing social critique is not exegetically grounded. The compatibility of this notion with social critique has indeed been shown to be possible and productive, for instance, in feminist perspectives (Scheman and O'Connor 2002; Scheman 2017).[45] Crucial to a notion of forms of life that allows for social critique is an idea of the relationship between practices and rules that allows for some sort of flexibility and reflexivity, going beyond the image of the agent as a blind rule follower.

3.4.2 Rules

The Wittgensteinian conception of rule following is another area in which the literature has interacted with a wider debate, in this case expanding to other fields such as sociology and ethnomethodology. Again, it is not my aim here to investigate this issue in depth, as it deserves much more than a few pages, but given its strict connection with forms of life, it is worth, I believe, providing a brief overview of it and its bearings on different interpretations of forms of life.

Following a rule is the central topic of *PI* §§185–242 according to most commentaries on *PI*.[46] The discussion opens with the example of a student learning to continue a series. After teaching a pupil to continue a series by adding +2, we discover that beyond 1,000, she writes 1,004, 1,008, and so forth instead of 1,002, 1,004, and so forth. In response to our perplexity, she claims that she understands the rule and our order perfectly – indeed, she is doing precisely what we asked her to do. In such a case, Wittgenstein observes, one might say that this person *finds it natural* to understand our order to add 2 the same way we would understand an order such as the following: add 2 up to

---

[45] See Jaeggi 2018 for a broader discussion.

[46] For instance, Baker and Hacker 2009; Biletzki and Matar 2021. Stern (2004: 139–70) identifies in *PI* §§134–242, the "third chapter" of the *Investigations*, in which the theme of rule following is a central concern.

1,000, then add 4 up to 2,000, then add 6 up to 3,000, and so forth (*PI* §185). However, the problem here is how are we to "rule out" her interpretation of the rule as mistaken? On the basis of what can we say that she should have continued the way *we* would have continued? No matter what justification we give, she will still be able to argue that she was following the rule correctly. She will appeal to her interpretation of the rule as the obvious and correct one. This is essentially what has been called the paradox of rule following, as summarized in *PI* §201:

> This was our paradox: no course of action could be determined by a rule, because every course of action can be brought into accord with the rule. The answer was: if every course of action can be brought into accord with the rule, then it can also be brought into conflict with it. And so there would be neither accord nor conflict here.

However, Wittgenstein continues, a misunderstanding is hidden in this formulation of the paradox – or perhaps a misunderstanding is at the origin of the very idea that a paradox exists here: we assumed that following a rule is always a matter of interpretation, and that behind each interpretation must be another interpretation, without realizing that "there is a way of grasping a rule which is *not* an interpretation" (*PI* §201); there is a way of grasping a rule that shows just in our applications of the rule and in what we are inclined to call following a rule and going against it. At bottom, following a rule is not an interpretation but a *practice*, and for a practice to be such, it cannot be private (*PI* §202).

What is the nature of this social practice that is supposed to clarify the relationship between rule and application? Two trends can be identified in the literature. On the one hand, there are those who emphasize that practices are ultimately conventions, and conventions can be stipulated, withdrawn, and changed. One example is Dummett, according to whom every step in the application of a rule involves a decision:

> Wittgenstein goes in for a full-blooded conventionalism: for him, the logical necessity of any statement is always the direct expression of a linguistic convention. That a given statement is necessary consists always in our having expressly decided to treat that very statement as unassailable.
>
> (Dummett 1959: 329)

In this view, in the end, logic and mathematics themselves belong to the realm of conventions. On the other hand, there are those who emphasize Wittgenstein's insistence on the fact that we follow rules blindly (*PI* §219), automatically, and without reflection and hence that our social norms have a compelling power over us. Kripke's (1982) influential reading of the "paradox" of rule following as a skeptical problem is an example.[47] For Kripke, the paradox shows that we cannot truly know what it means to follow a rule correctly. In his view, Wittgenstein acknowledges this and offers a skeptical solution to the skeptical problem: the only criterion we have for the correctness of rules is a social one. We are socially trained to follow rules in the way in which our community follows them. The rule therefore is an external (even if internalized) constraint to which we adhere as members of our community. Note that the two positions are not incompatible: one might claim that rules are arbitrary conventions *and* that we follow them blindly, constrained by our form of life.

What is left out in this view and more generally in what Crary (2000) calls "inviolability interpretations" of Wittgenstein's philosophy is some room for the *flexibility* of rules, which Wittgenstein actually defends. Even when he affirms that we follow rules blindly, Wittgenstein qualifies his statement, adding that he is speaking *symbolically*: he is giving expression to a symbol or a picture of what we mean by "rule." *According to this picture*, there is a rigidity in the rule, an inexorability, and our actions and practices are determined by it. However, this is *in the picture* of the rule that we have. Let us consider the remark on following a rule blindly in its context:

> "All the steps are really already taken" means: I no longer have any choice. The rule, once stamped with a particular meaning, traces the lines along which it is to be followed through the whole of space. – But if something of this sort really were the case, how would it help me?
>
> No; my description made sense only if it was to be understood symbolically. – I should say: *This is how it strikes me.*
>
> When I follow the rule, I do not choose.
>
> I follow the rule *blindly*.
>
> (*PI* §219)

The picture of a rule that Wittgenstein is describing (not endorsing) here derives from what he calls "the machine as symbol":

> A machine as a symbol of its mode of operation. The machine, I might say for a start, seems already to contain its own mode of operation. What does that mean? If we know the machine, everything else – that is the movements it will make – seems to be already completely determined.
>
> (*PI* §193, see also *RFM*: 84–85)

Wittgenstein observes that we talk of the machine as if its parts could move only in a certain way, but we do not consider that parts might break down, melt, or bend; when we are seduced by the picture of the machine, we use it as a symbol of a mode of operation without considering the movements of a real

---
[47] See also Fogelin 1976.

material machine. The same picture seems to be operating in the idea of rules as rigid, similar to rails, and us following them blindly, similar to a train on rails. However, this is a picture that we make for ourselves, especially when philosophizing, and like most philosophical pictures, it can lead us astray (*PI* §194).

When we think about meaning, still seduced by this picture, we tend to think of grasping the whole meaning of a word in a flash, as if its future developments, with their rules of use, were already mysteriously present in our understanding (*PI* §197). Therefore, when we ask ourselves, "How can a rule teach me what I have to do at *this* point?," we seem to end up in a puzzle because we seek an interpretation of the rule, but "interpretations by themselves do not determine meaning" (*PI* §198). Where is the connection, then, between an order or a sign and our action?

> Well, this one, for example: I have been trained to react in a particular way to this sign, and now I do so react to it. . . . [A] person goes by a signpost only in so far as there is an established usage, a custom. (*PI* §198)

One might wonder how this idea is different from the picture of the rails or the machine. The point, as I see it, is that in addition to involving a community, a practice or a custom requires mastering a technique; allows for the possibility of variations, alterations, and remodulations; and does not preclude critique. In contrast to the predetermined movements of a "machine as symbol," a practice is a human affair; it is embedded within a social and historical context and can shift through time. A practice involves a form of life.[48]

That rules make sense only in the context of a form of life also means that they can evolve and change (unlike "machines as symbols"). Even if rules channel actions, actions, such as the movements of the waters, can influence the trajectory of the river (cf. *OC* §§95–99). This does not abolish the distinction between rule and action (or between the logical and the empirical, as Wittgenstein puts it in *OC*); rather, it captures the flexibility of their relationship and the incompleteness of rules (*OC* §139).

Wittgenstein's considerations about rule following as a custom or a practice, then, help us see at the same time the depth and the contingency of forms of life, their fundamentality, and their permeability to change (Minar 2011; Colapietro 2011). By the same token, they make room for the possibility of criticism. Indeed, if the rule follower is not a blind automaton but an individual who has mastered a technique and acquired competences, they will also be able to evaluate the appropriateness of actions and rules themselves to contexts.

---

[48] It is fascinating to see how the comparison between machines and humans emerges in parallel in Wittgenstein's and Turing's thought. As noted earlier, indeed, it is very likely that the conversations between the two had some role in stimulating the Wittgensteinian notions of rules and forms of life. See Section 1 and Floyd 2016, 2018, 2020.

If rules have "loopholes" (*OC* §139), agents must master a sophisticated and complex reflexivity in order to know how to respond to unpredictable circumstances, how to extend norms to new cases, and how to adapt and change norms when needed (Celikates 2015). Additionally, the possibility of criticism is not necessarily limited to internal criticism, aimed only at ameliorating practices *given* a certain form of life. Rather, the encounter with other forms of life and different ways of doing, including the exercise of imagination in picturing alien forms of life, can equip one with tools for a form of immanent criticism that identifies contradictions and has transformative purposes.[49]

3.4.3 Naturalism

Another debate that characterizes the literature on forms of life and extends to wider issues concerns naturalism. In this case, the debate does not touch on political issues but connects with different conceptions of philosophy and the relationship between philosophy and the sciences. Focusing on this discussion therefore also provides a background for introducing the methodological reading of forms of life.

Recall the map of interpretations proposed in Section 3.3, organized around the three axes of debate: natural versus cultural, one versus many, and empirical versus transcendental. The last of these is the one that matters most here. Consider empirical interpretations of forms of life, namely, those claiming that the notion of *Lebensform* is intended to describe actual groups of people or societies and their linguistic practices as interwoven with their actions and customs. Viewing the Wittgensteinian notion as an example of Wittgenstein's descriptive and empirical attitude has led some to argue that Wittgenstein should be considered a naturalist offering an account of language and normativity based on the nature of human beings as complex organisms in their environment and more generally exemplifying a conception of philosophy itself as essentially aiming to replace metaphysical considerations with empirical or perhaps anthropological observations about what human beings do in their life.

What "naturalism" means in philosophy is itself subject to debate, and hence the claim that Wittgenstein is (or is not) a naturalist remains obscure unless a preliminary clarification of the meaning of naturalism is provided. Without attempting a complete definition, suffice it to say that generally, both those who claim that Wittgenstein was a naturalist and those who claim that he was not recognize that a naturalistic attitude implies perceiving some continuity between philosophy and science. At the same time, both acknowledge that

---

[49] I am referring here to the distinction between internal and immanent criticism put forth by Jaeggi 2018.

naturalism is not to be conflated with scientism, so if one is to talk about an alleged naturalism in Wittgenstein, it is not the reductive kind of naturalism that derives from a scientistic perspective. By scientism, I mean the idea that philosophy is not only contiguous to science but also should adopt its methods and goals and, in particular, should aim for a unified explanation of phenomena based on the model of the physical sciences. That Wittgenstein strongly opposed such a view is not contentious.

Granting that there can be a nonreductive form of naturalism, is Wittgenstein to be considered a naturalist? Many commentators argue as much. Marie McGinn (1989: 147), for instance, affirms that "the outlook of Wittgenstein's later philosophy is thoroughgoing naturalism." Her characterization of Wittgenstein's (alleged) naturalism is as follows:

> [T]he importance of seeing things in context, of looking at particular cases, of seeing connections, of looking at how something develops or unfolds in time and of recognizing patterns; the rejection of explanation in favor of descrip-tion; the use of analogies and comparisons; the suspicion of abstractions, hypostatizations, and idealizations; the avoidance of dogmas; the appeal to the reader's full sensuous awareness of phenomena and the attempt to make phenomena present to the imagination; and finally, the consistent emphasis on doing rather than knowing, on the application or employment of linguistic techniques in everyday, human activities and on the roots of our language-games in our primitive responses and reactions. (McGinn 2010: 347)

This view can be traced back to earlier thinkers who built on Wittgenstein to develop their own perspectives, such as Peter Strawson and John McDowell (though McGinn is here distancing herself from McDowell's view). Strawson describes Wittgenstein's perspective as a form of "social naturalism" (a precur-sor of Strawson's own liberal naturalism) in which the natural consists of what human beings learn as members of a community, and this is taken as "primi-tive," as needing no further explanation (Strawson 1985: 24, 78). McDowell (1994: 86, 92–95) proposes a "naturalism of second nature" in which the role of the *Bildung* assumes center stage and finds in Wittgenstein a forerunner of the same idea.

To remain more strictly within the Wittgensteinian literature, David Pears claims that Wittgenstein's privileging description over explanation is indeed a form of naturalism, a perspective that helps him deal with the issue of rule following. According to Pears (1995: 419), it is the naturalistic appeal to something extralinguistic, namely, "pre-existing independent structures," that allows Wittgenstein to dissolve the skeptical challenge in rule following in a move that deliberately trespasses on the territories of sociology and anthro-pology (see also Snowdon 2018). Baker and Hacker (2009: 220, 329) too, as we saw earlier, in a sense invoke a sort of naturalism when they highlight that continuing a series of numbers the way we do is something we find "culturally natural" or "natural in our culture." What these views generally point out is that Wittgenstein shows a naturalistic attitude toward human actions and practices while at the same time recognizing their intrinsic and irreducible normativity; his naturalism, in fact, remains antiscientistic and antireductionist (Smith 2017). McArthur (2018: 42) nicely summarizes what seems to be a common aim of these perspectives:

> Part of the point of calling Wittgenstein's method a form of naturalism is the importance it attaches to reminding us of the ordinary use of words as they function in the everyday lives of human beings considered as natural beings in a natural world – the relevant contrast being supernatural beings in a supernatural world.

In other words, in this view, Wittgenstein's naturalistic perspective is not a premise of a scientific explanation of phenomena but an antidote to the tendency to appeal to "the supernatural," or, we might say, to metaphysical entities.[50]

However, an empirical attitude that examines actual phenomena in order to answer a philosophical question is often, for Wittgenstein, not the way out of but the way *into* metaphysical troubles. Naturalistic interpretations of Wittgenstein therefore should be careful to also distinguish naturalism from an empirical investigation, if that is possible. This is perhaps what Wittgenstein is referring to when he claims, "Not empiricism and yet realism in philosophy, that is the hardest thing. (Against Ramsey)" (*RFM*: 325).

One occasion on which Wittgenstein clarifies this point is when he comments on the pragmatist idea that belief is an adjustment of the organism to its environment (attributed either to Dewey or to Russell; see *PGL*: 90, 219, 320). A question such as "What is belief?" can be taken in different senses, Wittgenstein observes: as an empirical question or a conceptual one. The problem is that we often ask such questions with a conceptual investigation in mind – we ask about the meaning of a word – but the question itself appears to be empirical; it seems that we are seeking an explanation of an actual phenomenon. However, if we are asking about the meaning of "belief," then examining empirical cases would not provide a satisfactory answer because an empirical investigation would at best offer a description of *some aspects* of this meaning. Taking these empirical findings as an answer to a conceptual question would lead to nothing but confusion. In the case of belief, it might be true that in some cases, for instance, cases involving expectations, when a subject believes that

---

[50] For more on Wittgenstein and naturalism, see Cahill and Raleigh 2018.

something is going to happen, the subject's organism prepares for that event (it adjusts to the environment, as Dewey or Russell might claim). This is an empirical hypothesis. However, answering the conceptual question "What is belief?" with this empirical claim, Wittgenstein argues, is simply wrong. One of Wittgenstein's students synthesized this argument as follows:

If I expect, my organism prepares. (Experiential.)
I expect = My organism prepares. (This is wrong.) (*PGL*: 219).

The first statement expresses an empirical hypothesis; the second one establishes or describes a meaning. What is at stake here is a distinction that permeates the whole of Wittgenstein's work; the distinction between an empirical and a logical (or grammatical, or conceptual) investigation. The latter, which is what Wittgenstein is interested in, must be undertaken by examining *the way in which we use the words* in question rather than facts. Alternatively, and better, one ought to look at facts only insofar as they are part of the contexts of the use of words and as such help us shed light on these uses. As he put it elsewhere,

> Philosophical investigations: conceptual investigations. The essential thing about metaphysics: that the difference between factual and conceptual investigations is not clear to it. A metaphysical question is always in appearance a factual one, although the problem is a conceptual one. (*RPP I* §949)

I am not sure that empirical accounts of forms of life and naturalistic interpretations of Wittgenstein's philosophy overall are able to save this distinction.

However, acknowledging that Wittgenstein is working on a conceptual rather than an empirical level and, more broadly, resisting a naturalistic interpretation of his work does not amount to an endorsement of a transcendental reading (which I previously contrasted with an empirical reading). Indeed, attention to the concrete (and imaginary) circumstances in which we tend to use certain words can and should be part of the conceptual investigation if it means clarifying contexts of use (rather than seeking empirical answers) and acknowledging "the ways in which the language we speak is contingent on the circumstances of our lives" (Hertzberg 2011: 351). Moreover, "conceptual" and "transcendental" are of course not synonyms; quite the opposite, an inquiry aimed at a synoptic view of our uses of words can actually be intended as an attempt to detranscendentalize concepts and bring them back to the ordinary. As I will argue in the concluding section, indeed, a *methodological* (rather than either an empirical or a transcendental) reading of forms of life allows one to preserve the conceptual nature of Wittgenstein's work as well as to recognize the fruitfulness and significance of this notion.

4 Conclusion: The Significance of Forms of Life

4.1 Overview

Sections 2 and 3 examined Wittgenstein's remarks on forms of life and the literature on forms of life, including some broader debates stimulated by this topic. Wittgenstein's remarks were grouped into three thematic clusters roughly corresponding to three different periods: observations concerning language games and the activities of life, agreement and rule following, and forms of life as the given. The examination of the literature allowed us to identify three main axes of debate: natural versus cultural readings, singular versus plural readings, and empirical versus transcendental readings. Further discussions briefly considered relativism and conservatism, rule following, and naturalism. In this concluding section, I combine the results of the former two, discussing whether any of the different positions in the map of interpretations is well suited to make sense of the totality of Wittgenstein's remarks on forms of life. Part of the difficulty, I argue, is due to Wittgenstein using this notion in slightly different ways through time. Finally, I will propose a methodological reading of forms of life that promises to make room for such variability and at the same time explain Wittgenstein's seeming reluctance to explain exactly what forms of life are in a substantive way.

4.2 Remarks and Interpretations

Are there readings among those examined that comprehensively capture the ways in which Wittgenstein uses the term "forms of life" in his writings and lectures? Recall the "natural versus cultural" axis of debate. Interpreters who claim that a form of life is something that characterizes human beings as natural organisms find themselves at ease with Wittgenstein's remarks about forms of life as primitive or foundational with respect to language games (for instance, *PO*: 397) or as reflecting "the common behavior of mankind" (*PI* §206), "the nature of our lives" (*WCL*: 234), or a sort of "animal certainty" (*OC* §§358–59) and with Wittgenstein's insistence on language games being part of our natural history, just as walking, eating, drinking, and playing are (*PI* §25). However, in several other passages, Wittgenstein seems to refer to cultural aspects; for instance, when he reflects about a form of life culminating in "an utterance of belief in a Last Judgment" (*LC*: 58), when he provides examples related to mathematics or to comparing colors or measuring time or lengths (*PGL*: 23–24), when he refers to social roles and authority (*RFM*: 352), and when he distinguishes animal forms of life from the human form of life on the basis of language (*PPF* §1 [xi 192]). On the other hand, supporters of the cultural view must, of course, explain Wittgenstein's frequent insistence on natural history and animal certainty; additionally, their reliance on the continuity between his talk of culture before 1936 and his talk of forms of life afterward fails to explain why he actually stopped using *Kultur* in favor of *Lebensformen*. If there is a continuity and forms of life are essentially culture, why did he need to introduce a new term?

If we look at the second axis of debate, the "one versus many" interpretations, we find again that the two opposing views both capture some uses of *Lebensformen* but have trouble explaining others. For instance, similar to the organic account, a "monistic" reading according to which there is only one human form of life finds support in passages where Wittgenstein talks about the common behavior of mankind or the human form of life as opposed to the animal form (for instance, when he observes that the phenomena of hope are "variations of this complicated form of life," *PPF* §1 [xi 192]). However, it needs to explain those passages in which forms of life are hardly distinguishable from language games, activities, or ways of doing things, such as when he speaks of *Lebensformen* as "steady ways of living" (*PO*: 397), when he uses religion as an example (*LC*: 58), when he positions forms of life in parallel with techniques (MS 180: 26r–27r), or when he talks of *"particular* forms of life and speech" (*RFM*: 414; my emphasis; see also MS 165: 110). Readings that emphasize the plurality of forms of life, conversely, must find a way to make sense of Wittgenstein's remarks on the (one and only) *human* form of life.

Finally, on the third axis of debate, the "empirical versus transcendental" readings, while it might seem prima facie that the transcendental reading is more speculative and often builds on alleged analogies between the early and late Wittgenstein rather than specific remarks on forms of life, proponents of this view might claim that it is actually backed by Wittgenstein's refraining from saying much about forms of life: if forms of life are acknowledged as transcendental, describing them would actually be not feasible. The open question with which Wittgenstein ends his reflection on imponderable evidence and the imaginary example of the lie detector might suggest such a reading. Are we truly able to imagine how our life would change if an automatic portable lie detector were available to us? All of the practices, habits, and competences related to expressing oneself and understanding others would be turned upside down, and the thinkability of such a hypothesis would itself be questionable (*LW II*: 95). This reading would also make sense of the examples of logically alien forms of life that Wittgenstein offers; these would be exercises in the transcendental limits of our own form of life. However, a transcendental reading would fail to account for the many occasions on which Wittgenstein seems to simply describe actual communities and practices. The latter are what the empirical interpretation of forms of life emphasizes. The empirical reading is in fact backed by Wittgenstein's anthropological observations and general descriptive attitude, for instance, in all the remarks in which he shows "things we humans do" and invites us to compare our ways of giving and following orders, greeting, naming and describing colors, measuring, dancing, and so forth with the ways other "tribes" do or might do the same things (examples are in *PGL*: 23–24, MS 165: 110, *RPP I* §628).

It seems clear, then, that none of the poles of the different axes of the debate can comprehensively make sense of the various facets of Wittgenstein's forms of life. One might object that the interpretations just considered are mere abstractions, and commentators actually would not position themselves at the extremes of the axes of debate but somewhere in the middle. Even though this might be true for some of them – particularly for the "natural versus cultural" axis, where, as we saw, many authors are ready to acknowledge the coexistence of natural and cultural elements in forms of life even if they stress one aspect over the other – the point remains that Wittgenstein seems to be talking about forms of life in different senses on different occasions. This is indeed probably the main reason why there are so many divergent interpretations of this notion. All readings seem to be correct if we limit the range of the Wittgensteinian remarks to some of them. What are we to make of this? Is it that Wittgenstein is simply contradictory and does not have a coherent notion of forms of life?

4.3 The Development of Wittgenstein's View

Let us return once more to the Wittgensteinian remarks. In Section 2, I grouped them into three thematic clusters and highlighted that these clusters roughly correspond to different periods of Wittgenstein's work. What I would like to suggest is that it is possible to detect an evolution in Wittgenstein's use of this notion: in different phases of his work, he seems to emphasize different aspects of it. Given that the term *Lebensform* was already widely in use in Wittgenstein's time and already had a variety of connotations, when Wittgenstein used it, he simply did not need to define its meaning. The meaning was already in plain view, *and it already had different facets.* What Wittgenstein did was employ this notion for his purposes without disputing the variety of shades of meaning associated with it. Then, depending on the way in which he understood his own philosophy and his own task as a philosopher, in different periods, he tended to emphasize some aspects rather than others.

The first cluster of remarks dates roughly to 1936–7. The theme that emerges here is the various activities and phenomena of life with their language games. This is the period in which Wittgenstein develops an anthropological approach, stimulated by the encounter with Sraffa and the parallel development of the two thinkers' respective methods, both centered on identifying simple cases or situations and making them increasingly complex by adding new elements. It is also the period of Wittgenstein's conversations with Turing and his (their) reflections on human computation and the limits of the picture of the "machine as symbol." The early remarks on forms of life are those in which Wittgenstein invites us to imagine the simple, or "primitive," language game of the builders, constituted only of orders containing the words "block," "pillar," "slab," and "beam," as well as other hypothetical languages; the only way in which we can truly imagine these cases, he observes, is by imagining a form of life in which they are embedded. The context or surroundings of actions and practices are what makes a language understandable. These surroundings are not exhausted by the notion of "culture" because they comprise everyday habitual practices and activities that are much more basic than the notion of culture suggests. The notion of forms of life is meant to aid us in imagining these surroundings. Language games make sense only as belonging to a form of life. Remarks written in this period tend to express a cultural (as opposed to a natural), pluralistic (as opposed to monistic) and empirical (as opposed to transcendental) view of forms of life if one wants to use the categories identified in the map of readings of Section 3.3.

The remarks grouped in the second cluster focus on agreement and rule following and were written approximately between 1938 and 1944. What emerges here is the grounding role of forms of life and at the same time their constituting a form of agreement among human beings in their community and, overall, in humankind. The concern is with the depth of agreement and yet its "conventional" nature in the peculiar sense of "conventional" that Wittgenstein accustoms us to: a sense in which agreement on forms of life is not to be equated with agreement in opinion, with something that can be stipulated and withdrawn arbitrarily. The depth of human beings' agreement has the fundamentality of language and the normativity of rules; at the same time, it is not a foundation as traditional foundationalism would have it. It is a bedrock of action and habit brought about by training and discipline, the sort of discipline with which we learn to calculate, measure, speak, draw inferences, and follow rules the way our community does. This bedrock, in its most basic features, is shared by human beings, and it is on this ground that we are able, at least to some extent, to understand foreign communities and interpret foreign languages. In this period, different notions of forms of life seem to coexist, but the tendency seems to be toward a natural and monistic view. It is a view, however, in which the "natural" comprises the linguistic and cultural features of the life of human beings, and different levels of agreement on forms of life are acknowledged (the agreement of the community and the agreement of humankind). Does this notion reflect an empirical or a transcendental outlook? The anthropological attention to facts of human life is still there, but the addition of imaginary examples has the effect of creating more distance between the observer and the observed and of pushing the analysis toward the limits of our shared form of life. I am not sure this movement can be characterized as a shift from an empirical toward a transcendental view (in fact, I am convinced that Wittgenstein's employment of the notion of forms of life is neither empirical nor transcendental in any of the phases we're examining), but I do discern a shift here, or perhaps a growth in the awareness of the kind of analysis Wittgenstein is performing. This is captured, for instance, in this remark, written in 1940:

> If we use the ethnological approach does that mean we are saying philosophy is ethnology? No it only means we are taking up our position far outside, in order to see the things *more objectively*. (*CV*: 45 [37])

The third cluster of remarks, written after the Second World War, revolves around the theme of the given. What emerges here is the fundamentality and inescapability of forms of life as the level at which philosophical analysis must stop. We saw already that the exhortation to accept forms of life as the given is intended not as a conservative refraining from social critique but as a methodological appeal to counter the temptation to explain forms of life by identifying simple undefinable and "specific" elements to place at the basis of a theory. In this set of remarks, Wittgenstein seems also to increasingly focus on the complexities and peculiarities of the human form of life, not only for its cultural aspects but also for subtleties in the expression and understanding of emotions and feelings. Indeed, we might say that his reflection works in parallel on both the theme of certainty and the theme of uncertainty. Regarding the former, the notion of forms of life is applied to the "animal certainty" on which we normally act without reflection and take for granted the hinges around which our life turns. Regarding the latter, Wittgenstein shows an increasing interest in what human life *with others* looks like, including the constitutive uncertainty and imponderable evidence characterizing our perception of others' feelings, intentions, and emotions. In both cases, the notion of form of life is an invitation to see all this as primitive and to stop the philosophical temptation to seek a beginning *before* the beginning (*OC* §471). In this third phase, the notion of forms of life continues to include both cultural and natural elements; it is usually focused on the human form of life (hence, it is more compatible with a monistic approach than a pluralistic one), and it might seem to imply a transcendental tone. As I see it, this is in line with the overall trajectory of Wittgenstein's thought, which in the final years is reminiscent of some aspects of his early period, although in a totally different setting. In *OC*, logic, again, in a sense cannot be described, but what Wittgenstein is concerned with is the "logic in action" (cf. Moyal-Sharrock 2003) of our linguistic practices embedded in our form of life. As he puts it in *OC* §501, "Am I not getting closer and closer to saying that in the end logic cannot be described? You must look at the practice of language, then you will see it."

4.4 A Methodological Reading

I have argued that an evolution is detectable in Wittgenstein's employment of "forms of life," extending roughly from his anthropological attention to the concrete praxiological contexts of language games in different communities to a progressive focus on the human form of life and its limits. However, throughout his whole body of work, Wittgenstein never seems interested in a substantive notion of forms of life. He never defines it and never offers a comprehensive description of it. This is at least in part due to the fact that such an expression was already widely used at that time, as was highlighted in Section 1. When Wittgenstein uses this notion, it is usually for the purpose of highlighting something else, in particular, the embeddedness of our linguistic activities in wider praxeological surroundings and the relevance of keeping such surroundings in mind if we are to understand language. Ultimately, in my view, for Wittgenstein, the notion of forms of life is a methodological tool. The methodological nature of forms of life is also something that emerges progressively, becoming clearer in the last period of Wittgenstein's work. The remark on forms of life as the given embodies in the clearest possible way this methodological sense of forms of life. The point is that if philosophy is essentially an investigation into meanings and the workings of our language, we need to look at the uses we make of words, and the uses we make of words can be properly seen only against the background of forms of life. Forms of life, however, provide the proper terrain for the description, not the causal explanation, of what we do with words. In fact, forms of life are "the given," and the philosophical temptation to go beyond this concept and explain it is something we should be wary of. Thus, the notion of forms of life tells us something about the nature and limits of philosophy itself.

By claiming that "forms of life" is a tool or an instrument for Wittgenstein's grammatical investigations, however, I do not mean to downplay the relevance of this notion. Quite the opposite. Hacker (2015: 18) claims that "the expression 'form of life' plays a very small role in Wittgenstein's later philosophy" and that this notion "in itself is of no great moment": it is simply part of a larger body of thought, that is, Wittgenstein's ethnological conception of language as embedded in the ways of living of a language-using community. In itself, Hacker argues, this notion is "merely a surface ornament" (18). While I agree that this notion is clearly part of a larger body of thought, I also believe that it plays quite an important role, and rightly so. As a methodological tool, it is an essential pointer that guides the philosopher's gaze in the right direction and a reminder of the scope and limits of a philosophical investigation.

Far from providing an empirical account of forms of life, but also far from proposing a substantive ethnological conception of language, as Hacker claims, Wittgenstein is engaged in a grammatical investigation that highlights the interconnectedness between our speaking a language and our being the particular animals that we are, agreeing in language and belonging to communities "bound together by science and education" (*OC* §298). In his words,

> [O]ur investigation is directed not towards *phenomena*, but rather, as one might say, towards the '*possibilities*' of phenomena. What that means is that we call to mind the *kinds of statement* that we make about phenomena. ...
> Our inquiry is therefore a grammatical one. And the inquiry sheds light on our problem by clearing misunderstandings away. (*PI* §90)

To reiterate, forms of life are not an object of investigation but a tool for grammatical investigations. As other commentators have also pointed out, the remark about the given "is a remark about philosophical method and the place in it for 'the given,'" where the given is not intended as a foundation in the traditional sense (Lagerspetz 2020: 122, 125). The appeal to accept forms of life as the given is an appeal for philosophers to take forms of life as a methodological starting point for their analyses, "accepting that our life with words is the place to look to resolve philosophical perplexity" (Witherspoon 2003: 230) and recognizing how our language is contingent on the circumstances we find ourself living in (Hertzberg 2011: 351). In Floyd's words (2020: 116), the notion of forms of life "is not an anthropological fact or given culture to be described, but rather a norm of elucidation and of characterization. It earmarks a new philosophical and critical method, a method which we can now see as an important innovation in the history of philosophy in the 20th century."

The methodological reading of forms of life is confirmed if we look back at Wittgenstein's criticism of Spengler, which we touched on at the end of Section 1. Wittgenstein, as we saw, took inspiration from Spengler in the development of his method of synoptic presentation and the notion of forms of life but was well aware of some risks involved in Spengler's view. These risks are related to conflation of the "prototype" (a methodological tool) with the object of the investigation. As early as 1931, he commented on Spengler:

We have to be told the object of comparison, the object from which this approach is derived, so that prejudices do not constantly slip into the discussion. . . . But since we confuse prototype & object we find ourselves dogmatically conferring on the object properties which only the prototype necessarily possesses. On the other hand we think the approach will lack the generality we want to give it if it really holds only of the one case. But the prototype must just be presented for what it is; as characterizing the whole approach and determining its form. In this way it stands at the head & is generally valid by virtue of determining the form of approach, not by virtue of a claim that everything which is true only of it holds for all the objects to which the approach is applied. (*CV*: 21–22 [14])

The prototype then the methodological notion, is valid as an object of comparison but is not itself the object of the investigation.[51] If we were to define the features of the prototype and try to find them in the features of the phenomena we are investigating, we would be falling prone to a philosophical temptation: "our craving for generality," one source of which is our tendency to imitate the methods of science (*BBB*: 17, 18). This was clear for Wittgenstein from the beginning of the 1930s (if not earlier). With the later notion of forms of life, he not only keeps faith with this early warning but also further develops it into a warning against the philosophical temptation to try to reach a beginning before the beginning (*OC* §471) or to try to reach a ground beyond the ground that we already have in front of us.

The difficult thing here is not, to dig down to the ground; no, it is to recognize the ground that lies before us as the ground.
    For the ground keeps on giving us the illusory image of a greater depth, and when we seek to reach this, we keep on finding ourselves on the old level.
    Our disease is one of wanting to explain. (*RFM*: 333)

If this reading is correct, referring to forms of life in a philosophical inquiry does not amount to claiming that philosophers should study forms of life – for instance, analyzing the ways we behave with each other in different cultural contexts, or discovering the commonalities among different social groups and perhaps the features that characterize all human beings as such, and so forth. Rather, keeping in mind the conceptual and grammatical nature of the Wittgensteinian approach, referring to forms of life means indicating the terrain where meanings obtain their life and hence the place where a better understanding of such meanings is achievable. Showing how words are used *in forms of life* at multiple levels (from the immediate practical context to the wider social and cultural framework and ultimately

---

[51] Note that Wittgenstein applies the same criticism also to himself; see *PI* §§ 104, 114, 130–31, and Kuusela 2022: 25–27.

the human way of living) is instrumental in obtaining a clearer grasp of the grammar, the implications, and perhaps also the contradictions of our meanings. Forms of life in this sense constitute a reminder for philosophers about the nature of their job. As such, it is also a reminder aimed to the avoidance of metaphysics. Metaphysics, as Wittgenstein sees it, results not only from the temptation of abstract and context-free thinking but also from the attempt to answer a conceptual question through empirical means (*RPP I* §499). At the same time, using forms of life as a tool rather than examining forms of life as an object of study allows philosophers to also neutralize the temptation of science, that is, the tendency to interpret their work as the construction of a body of knowledge based on empirical observation and verification (*BBB*: 17–18). Philosophy for Wittgenstein seems much more concerned with a form of understanding than of knowledge. To put it in a slogan, forms of life are an instrument that helps deepen our understanding rather than increase our knowledge.

What I have highlighted so far is the use of forms of life as a tool in a metaphilosophical reflection and in the practice of philosophy itself. We can think of the job that "forms of life" performs at this level as similar to the job of signs on rocks and trees that help the hiker stay on track, keeping away from apparently easy shortcuts as well as from hidden cliffs, traps, and dead ends. Looking at forms of life to deepen our understanding of meanings is a way for "assembling reminders for a particular purpose" (*PI* §127; in Anscombe's translation), exploring or rediscovering the familiar paths of everyday life as opposed to either climbing on metaphysical systems or sliding into empirical research and scientific explanations.

Besides these metaphilosophical considerations, there are also other areas of thought in which this concept can be put to use. I conclude by considering two more ways in which such a tool can be used productively: political reflection, and ethical/aesthetical "exercises."

Regarding the relationship between philosophy and broadly political reflection, I am expanding on the debates about conservatism and relativism and about rules dealt with in Sections 3.4.1 and 3.4.2. Acknowledging that Wittgenstein is not proposing forms of life as the subject matter of analysis, but as a terrain or an environment for conceptual investigations and the cultivation of understanding amounts to making room for an exploration of the possibilities of our life with words, which, in broadly political terms, can take many forms and have multiple aims. I am going to highlight two aspects that in my view are particularly relevant.

On the one hand, such an approach is an appeal to never lose touch with the concreteness of situations, an appeal then against idealization and in favor of a political reflection anchored in a realistic attitude. This approach pays attention to the actual possibilities that open up in the dialectic between tradition and change, that is, between rule and practice. As we have seen, a Wittgensteinian understanding of rule-following helps highlight not only the constraints that a rule poses on practices, but also the role played by the agents' competences and their capacity to master and adapt rules to new and evolving situations. The "givenness" of forms of life in this context calls for the recognition of both the normative force of rules and the lived and enacted options of competent agents and communities manifesting in the plasticity of practices. A political reflection stemming from this approach hence recognizes the normative force of tradition without thereby resulting in a form of conservatism – conversely, at least potentially, it can also identify sites for shifts, reform, and change.

On the other hand, the notion of forms of life encourages an exploration of political *conceptual possibilities*. It is a matter of *concepts* because this is the terrain of philosophy, for Wittgenstein, as here highlighted: the connection between language games and forms of life (*PI* §23) emphasizes that only by reference to forms of life can we grasp what our words are about. And it is a matter of *possibilities* because the array of the Wittgensteinian examples of forms of life is an invitation to look at not only our actual everyday life but also at possible alterations of it (extensions, mutilations, or modifications of parts), as well as at nonfamiliar, foreign, and alien ways of living, with their possibly nonfamiliar, foreign, and alien concepts. The notion of forms of life, especially when we think about Wittgenstein's imaginary examples, emerges once more as a tool for thinking, and when it comes to a broadly political reflection, it translates into an attitude of conceptual openness that instead of judging other ways of living based on given meanings, *uses* other (real or imagined) ways of living for a rethinking of meanings.

He once complained about Ramsey because he saw him as a "bourgeois thinker," interested in "clearing up the affairs of some particular community" rather than reflecting on other possibilities:

> The idea that this state might not be the only possible one partly disquieted him and partly bored him. He wanted to get down as quickly as possible to reflecting on the foundations – of *this* state. This was what he was good at & what really interested him; whereas real philosophical reflection disquieted him until he put its result (if it had one) on one side as trivial. (*CV*: 24 [17])[52]

In this light, even when the focus is on our own life with words, our gaze is informed by a broader horizon that helps us see the familiar as unfamiliar, worth

---

[52] Recall that Ramsey was also his polemical target when he claimed that the "hardest thing" in philosophy was achieving a form of realism and *not* of empiricism (*RFM*: 325).

attention, even uncanny sometimes (think, for instance, of Wittgenstein's notes about how we smile at a photograph [*RPP I* §1018], or about the coronation of a king [*PPF* §348 [xi 193]]).

Seeing forms of life as a tool in this sense helps overcome the tendency to discuss the political significance of Wittgenstein's thought in terms of interpretations of *his* political views as conservative or progressive or as having possible relativistic implications. It shifts the conversation instead toward another level, namely, the usability of his notions for what we might call political imagination. To put it in a slogan again, once forms of life are intended as a tool rather than an object of investigation, referring to forms of life in political reflection is not a conversation stopper, but a conversation *starter*: it opens up the terrain to debates informed by conceptual explorations.[53]

Finally, the points made about metaphilosophy and political thought suggest a third and wider area in which the methodological reading of forms of life proves useful: this is what I called above "ethical/aesthetical exercises." Indeed, the same kind of imaginative explorations that the notion of forms of life solicits in metaphilosophy and political thought can interest us on a more personal level, as exercises aimed at developing one's own capacity to see the limits of one's concepts and to imagine alternative possibilities. Rethinking our concepts in the light of their embeddedness in our form of life, stretching our meanings by envisioning and "trying out" altered environments for them enables an exercise in self-examination and self-criticism with possible transformative outcomes.[54] The realization that this might bring about is that certain limits that one saw in reality were actually limits in one's own conceptual repertoire, and once room is made for an even slight shift in our concepts, other aspects or possibilities become visible and practicable.

Wittgenstein often talks of "prejudices" when referring to preconceptions and habits of thought that are difficult to dislodge. In *PI* §340 for instance, he observes:

> One cannot guess how a word functions. One has to look at its application and learn from that.
>   But the difficulty is to remove the prejudice [*Vorurteil*] which stands in the way of doing so. It is not a *stupid* prejudice.

---

[53] Talk of imagining possible alterations of our concept brings to mind the contemporary perspective of conceptual engineering (Burgess et al. 2020). It would be fascinating to delve into a Wittgensteinian understanding of this approach. Though I cannot expand on this topic here, suffice it to say that, while the idea of modifying our concepts "from above," as it were, sounds obviously quite un-Wittgensteinian, investigations into the historical development of concepts, the connections between concepts and their environment, and the social implications of concepts would surely benefit from a Wittgensteinian outlook.

[54] There are some similarities here with pragmatism, especially with William James's ethical attitude (cf. Boncompagni 2016a: chapter 6 and conclusion).

Removing these nonstupid prejudices is the aim of Wittgenstein's philosophy, and the notion of forms of life is a tool in the service of such aim, a tool for the enlargement and strengthening of philosophical imagination. Note the moral tone that is implicit in this talk of prejudices, a moral tone that one can read, both explicitly and between the lines, in many Wittgensteinian reflections on the difficulties of the philosopher (Morris 2007). The struggle to eliminate philosophical prejudices, identifying and possibly neutralizing linguistic traps and captivating pictures that keep our mind "pressing against a blank wall" (*BBB*: 169), for Wittgenstein, is a *moral* one.[55]

The ethical implications of a work on prejudices of thinking, even if one does not share the (maybe) overly moral attitude of Wittgenstein's own way of taking philosophical work in general, emerges most clearly by considering the implications in the social world. Looking at forms of life becomes especially salient when one examines all those categories by which we organize, manage, and discipline our lives with others: concepts and practices of authority, the family, relationships, social identities, social structures, economic exchanges, laws, obligations, rites (not to mention all that relates to religion, culture, science, and education). Seeing the connections between words and forms of life makes one aware of the *normativity* and *contingency* of social categories, their constraining power *and* their plasticity; training oneself in this awareness is a way for exercising and improving one's sensibility to possible alternatives. Regarding social concepts that categorize people and forms of social life, such a sensibility results in the capacity to harken, hear, and possibly understand – or at least give room to – alternative ways of living, in which the salience of certain concepts and practices may be different from the usual one.[56] Again, I do not claim that Wittgenstein was (or was not) a good practitioner of this sort of social sensibility. Rather, I am claiming that making use of his conceptual tools can help one become a good practitioner.

Note that this sensibility is, in a sense, both an ethical and an aesthetic one if we think of aesthetics as an exercise and perfecting of attention. I mentioned earlier (Section 2.4) the expert knowledge of human beings (*Menschenkenntnis*) that Wittgenstein refers to when dealing with imponderable evidence (*PPF* §355 [xi 193]), an expert knowledge that is part of the effort to *hear* others. The expert judgment of the genuineness of expressions of feeling, Wittgenstein notes, is of the same kind as the expert judgment of the authorship of a work of art, and more generally of the quality of a work of art; one has to "get an eye" for

---

[55] On captivating (but also liberating) pictures, see Boncompagni, in press.

[56] To use another vocabulary, one might talk here of a sensibility to the voices of the marginalized, and of the capacity to become active listeners, in what Miranda Fricker would call the virtue of hermeneutical justice (cf. Fricker 2007: chapter 7).

it (a "nose" in the previous translation; *PPF* §361 [xi 194]) – for recognizing the meaningfulness of certain gestures or the significance of certain strokes on a canvas. Only within a whole world saturated with human and cultural meanings can gestures, like strokes on a canvas, express ideas with subtleties and nuances and be understood (and misunderstood). Once again, the appeal to forms of life is a reminder that calls for acknowledging where, how, and in virtue of what words (gestures, brush strokes) are meaningful.

To conclude, a methodological reading of forms of life that considers this notion as a tool rather than an object of investigation, in my view, allows us to appreciate Wittgenstein's overall metaphilosophy as well as the significance of his thought for political reflection and more broadly for conceptual exercises aimed at the cultivation of a certain kind of (ethical and aesthetic) sensitivity.[57] This is not the only conceptual tool Wittgenstein elaborates; other examples include the notions of family resemblances, language games, synoptic or surveyable representation, meaning as use, and hinges. Without denying that these notions tell us something about "the workings of our language" (*PI* §109), they are best seen as instruments that help shed light on such workings by way of improving our understanding, skills of thinking, and sensitivity.

---

[57] On the notion of "exercises" in Wittgenstein, see Guidi, in press.

References

Abreu e Silva Netu, N. (2011). "The Uses of 'Forms of Life' and the Meanings of Life," in J. Padilla Gálvez and M. Gaffal, eds., *Forms of Life and Language Games*, Berlin: Ontos Verlag, 75–106.

Ammann, H. (1928). *Die menschliche Rede: Sprachphilosophische Einrichtungen*, vol. 2, *Lebensform und Lebensfunktionen der Rede*, Moritz Schauenburg: Lahr.

Andronico. M. (1999). "Morphology in Wittgenstein," in R. Egidi, ed., *In Search of a New Humanism*, Dordrecht. Springer, 57–102.

Arena, R. (2013). "Sraffa's and Wittgenstein's Reciprocal Influences: Forms of Life and Snapshots," in E. S. Levrero, A. Palumbo, and A. Stirati, eds., *Sraffa and the Reconstruction of Economic Theory*, vol. 3, London: Palgrave Macmillan, 84–105.

Avins, S. (2014). "Brahms in the Wittgenstein Homes: A Memoir and Letters," in K. Hamilton and N. Loges, eds., *Brahms in the Home and the Concert Hall: Between Private and Public Performance*, Cambridge: Cambridge University Press, 221–55.

Baker, G. P. and Hacker, P. M. S. (2005 [1980]). *Wittgenstein: Understanding and Meaning: Volume 1 of An Analytical Commentary on the Philosophical Investigations*, Oxford: Blackwell.

Baker, G. P. and Hacker, P. M. S. (2009 [1985]). *Wittgenstein: Rules, Grammar and Necessity: Volume 2 of An Analytical Commentary on the Philosophical Investigations*, Oxford: Blackwell.

Biletzki, A. and Matar, A. (2021). "Ludwig Wittgenstein," in Edwarde N. Zalta, ed., *The Stanford Encyclopedia of Philosophy* (winter 2021 ed.), https://plato.stanford.edu/archives/win2021/entries/wittgenstein (accessed January 10, 2022).

Black, M. (1978). "*Lebensform* and *Sprachspiel* in Wittgenstein's Later Work," in A. Hübner, E. Leinfellner, H. Berghel, and W. Leinfellner, eds., *Wittgenstein and His Impact on Contemporary Philosophy: Proceedings of the 2nd International Wittgenstein Symposium*, Vienna: Hölder-Pichler-Tempsky, 325–31.

Boncompagni, A. (2015). "Elucidating Forms of Life: The Evolution of a Philosophical Tool," in D. Moyal-Sharrock and P. Donatelli, eds., "Wittgenstein and Forms of Life," special issue, *Nordic Wittgenstein Review*, 155–75.

Boncompagni, A. (2016a) *Wittgenstein and Pragmatism: On Certainty in the Light of Peirce and James*, Basingstoke: Palgrave Macmillan.

Boncompagni, A. (2016b). "'I'll Show you Something We Humans Do': Facts of Life in Wittgenstein and Peirce," *Paradigmi: Rivista di Filosofia*, 34(3), 51–65.

Boncompagni, A. (2018). "Immediacy and Experience in Wittgenstein's Notion of Imponderable Evidence," *Pragmatism Today*, 9(2), 94–106.

Boncompagni, A. (2019). "Wittgenstein and William James," in A. Klein, ed., *The Oxford Handbook of William James*, online ed., Oxford: Oxford University Press, https://doi.org/10.1093/oxfordhb/9780199395699.013.26.

Boncompagni, A. (in press). "Between Captivity and Liberation: The Role of Pictures in Wittgenstein's Philosophy," in L. Guidi, ed. *Wittgensteinian Exercises: Aesthetic and Ethical Transformations*, Paderborn: Fink/Brill.

Breithaupt, F., Raatzsch, R., and Kremberg, B., eds. (2003). *Goethe and Wittgenstein: Seeing the World's Unity in Its Variety*. Frankfurt: Peter Lang.

Burdach, K. F. (1838). *Die Physiologie der Erfahrungswissenschaft*, vol. 3 (1826–40), Leipzig: Voss.

Burgess, A., Cappelen, H., and Plunkett, D., eds. (2020). *Conceptual Engineering and Conceptual Ethics*, Oxford: Oxford University Press.

Cahill, K. M., and Raleigh, T., eds. (2018). *Wittgenstein and Naturalism*, London: Routledge.

Canfield, J. (1975). "Anthropological Science Fiction and Logical Necessity," *Canadian Journal of Philosophy*, 4(3), 467–79.

Cavell, S. (1962). "The Availability of Wittgenstein's Later Philosophy," *The Philosophical Review*, 71(1), 67–93.

Cavell, S. (1979). *The Claim of Reason*, Oxford: Oxford University Press.

Cavell, S. (1988). "Declining Decline: Wittgenstein as a Philosopher of Culture," *Inquiry*, 31(3), 253–64.

Cavell, S. (2004a) "The *Investigations*' Everyday Aesthetics of Itself," in J. Gibson and W. Huemer, eds., *The Literary Wittgenstein*, London: Routledge, 1–33.

Cavell, S. (2004b) "Postscript to 'The *Investigations*' Everyday Aesthetics of Itself,'" in M. De Caro and D. Macarthur, eds., *Naturalism in Question*, Cambridge, MA: Harvard University Press, 275–79.

Celikates, R. (2015). "Against Manichaeism: The Politics of Forms of Life and the Possibilities of Critique," *Raisons Politiques*, 57(1), 81–96.

Colapietro, V. (2011). "Allowing our Practices to Speak for Themselves: Wittgenstein, Peirce, and Their Intersecting Lineages," in R. M. Calcaterra, ed., *New Perspectives on Pragmatism and Analytic Philosophy*, Amsterdam: Rodopi/Brill, 1–20.

Coliva, A. (2010). "Was Wittgenstein an Epistemic Relativist?," *Philosophical Investigations*, 33(1), 1–23.

Conway, G. D. (1989). *Wittgenstein on Foundations*. Atlantic Highlands, NJ: Humanities Press.

Crary, A. (2000). "Wittgenstein's Philosophy in Relation to Political Thought," in A. Crary and R. Read, eds., *The New Wittgenstein*, London: Routledge.

Davis, J. B. (1988). "Sraffa, Wittgenstein and Neoclassical Economics," *Cambridge Journal of Economics*, 12, 29–36.

Davis, J. B. (1993). "Sraffa, Interdependence and Demand: The Gramscian Influence," *Review of Political Economy*, 5(1), 22–39.

Dummett, M. (1959). "Wittgenstein's Philosophy of Mathematics," *The Philosophical Review*, 68, 324–48.

Emmett, K. (1990). "Forms of Life," *Philosophical Investigations*, 13(3), 213–31.

Engelmann, M. (2013). "Wittgenstein's 'Most Fruitful Ideas' and Sraffa," *Philosophical Investigations*, 36(2), 155–78.

Floyd, J. (2016). "Chains of Life: Turing, *Lebensform*, and the Emergence of Wittgenstein's Later Style," *Nordic Wittgenstein Review*, 5(2), 7–89.

Floyd, J. (2018). "*Lebensform*: Living Logic," in C. Martin, ed., *Language, Form(s) of Life, and Logic*, Berlin: De Gruyter, 59–92.

Floyd, J. (2020). "Wittgenstein on Ethics: Working through *Lebensformen*," *Philosophy and Social Criticism*, 46(2), 115–30.

Fogelin, R. J. (1976). *Wittgenstein*, London: Routledge & Kegan Paul.

Fred, W. [Alfred Wechsler] (1905). *Lebensformen: Anmerkungen über die Technik des gesellschaftlichen Lebens*, Leipzig: Georg Müller.

Fricker, M. (2007). *Epistemic Injustice: Power and the Ethics of Knowing*, Oxford: Oxford University Press.

Gaffal, M. (2011). "Forms of Life as Social Techniques," in J. Padilla Gálvez and M. Gaffal, eds., *Forms of Life and Language Games*, Berlin: Ontos Verlag, 57–74.

Garver, N. (1984). "Die Lebensform in Wittgensteins Philosophischen Untersuchungen," *Grazer Philosophische Studien*, 21(1), 33–54.

Garver, N. (1994). "Naturalism and Transcendentality: The Case of 'Form of Life,'" in S. Teghrarian, ed., *Wittgenstein and Contemporary Philosophy*, Bristol: Thoemmes, 41–69.

Gellner, E. (1998). *Language and Solitude: Wittgenstein, Malinowski and the Habsburg Dilemma*, Cambridge: Cambridge University Press.

Gibson, A. and Mahony, N., eds. (2020). *Ludwig Wittgenstein: Dictating Philosophy*, Cham: Springer.

Gier, N. (1980). "Wittgenstein and Forms of Life," *Philosophy of the Social Sciences*, 10(3), 241–58.

Glock, H.-J. (1996). *A Wittgenstein Dictionary*, Oxford: Blackwell.

Goethe, J. W. von (1946 [1790]). "The Metamorphosis of Plants," in A. Arber, ed., *Goethe's Botany: The Metamorphosis of Plants (1790) and Tobler's Ode to Nature (1782)*, Waltham, MA: Chronica Botanica.

Guidi, L. ed. (in press). *Wittgensteinian Exercises: Aesthetic and Ethical Transformations*, Paderborn: Fink/Brill.

Hacker, P. M. S. (2015). "Forms of Life," in D. Moyal-Sharrock and P. Donatelli, eds., "Wittgenstein and Forms of Life," special issue, *Nordic Wittgenstein Review*, 1–20.

Haeckel, E. H. P. A. (1866). *Generelle Morphologie der Organismen*, Berlin: Reimer.

Haeckel, E. H. P. A. (1868). *Natürliche Schöpfungsgeschichte: Gemeinverständliche Wissenschaftliche*, Berlin: Reimer.

Haller, R. (2014). "Form of Life or Forms of Life? A Note on N. Garver's 'The Form of Life in Wittgenstein's Philosophical Investigations,'" in *Questions on Wittgenstein*, 2nd ed., London: Routledge, 129–36.

Hallett, G. (1977). *A Companion to Wittgenstein's 'Philosophical Investigations,'* Ithaca, NY: Cornell University Press.

Helmreich, S. and Roosth, S. (2010). "Life Forms: A Keyword Entry," *Representations*, 112(1), 27–53.

Hertzberg, L. (2011). "Very General Facts of Nature," in O. Kuusela and M. McGinn, eds., *The Oxford Handbook of Wittgenstein*, Oxford: Oxford University Press, 351–72.

Huizinga, J. (1924). *Waning of Middle Ages: A Study of the Forms of Life, Thought and Art in France and the Netherlands in the 14th and 15th Centuries*, London: The Whitefriars Press.

Hunter, J. F. M. (1968). "'Forms of Life' in Wittgenstein's *Philosophical Investigations*," *American Philosophical Quarterly*, 5(4), 233–43.

Jaeggi. R. (2018). *Critique of Forms of Life*, Cambridge, MA: Harvard University Press.

Janik A. and Toulmin, S. (1973). *Wittgenstein's Vienna*, New York: Simon and Schuster.

Kripke, S. (1982). *Wittgenstein on Rules and Private Language: An Elementary Exposition*, Oxford: Blackwell.

Kusch, M. (2013). "Annalisa Coliva on Wittgenstein and Epistemic Relativism," *Philosophia*, 41(1), 37–49.

Kusch, M. (2021). "Disagreement, Certainties, Relativism," *Topoi*, 40, 1097–105.

Kuusela, O. (2022). *Wittgenstein on Logic and Philosophical Method*, Cambridge: Cambridge University Press.

Lagerspetz, O. (2020). "Wittgenstein's Forms of Life: A Tool of Perspicuous Representation," *Nordic Wittgenstein Review*, 9, 107–31.

Lear, J. (1984). "The Disappearing 'We,'" *Proceedings of the Aristotelian Society, Supplementary Volumes*, 58, 219–42.

Malcolm, N. (1982). "Wittgenstein and Idealism," *Royal Institute of Philosophy Supplement*, 13, 249–67.

Malcolm, N. (2001 [1958]). *Ludwig Wittgenstein: A Memoir*, 2nd ed., Oxford: Clarendon.

Marcuse, H. (1991 [1964]). *One Dimensional Man*, 2nd ed., London: Routledge.

McArthur, D. (2018). "Wittgenstein's Liberal Naturalism of Human Nature," in K. M. Cahill and T. Raleigh, eds., *Wittgenstein and Naturalism*, London: Routledge, 33–55.

McDowell, J. (1994). *Mind and World*, Cambridge, MA: Harvard University Press.

McGinn, M. (1989). *Sense and Certainty*, Oxford: Blackwell.

McGinn, M. (2010). "Wittgenstein's Naturalism," in M. De Caro and D. Macarthur, eds., *Naturalism and Normativity*, New York: Columbia University Press, 322–51.

McGuinness, B., ed. (2012) *Wittgenstein in Cambridge: Letters and Documents 1911–1951*, 4th ed., Oxford: Blackwell.

McGuinness, B., ed. (2019). *Wittgenstein's Family Letters: Corresponding with Ludwig*, trans. P. Winslow, London: Bloomsbury.

Medina, J. (2003). "On Being Other-Minded: Wittgenstein, Davidson and Logical Aliens," *International Philosophical Quarterly*, 43(3), 463–75.

Minar, E. (2011). "The Life of the Sign. Rule-following, Practice, and Agreement," in O. Kuusela and M. McGinn, eds., *The Oxford Handbook of Wittgenstein*, Oxford: Oxford University Press, 276–93.

Morris, K. (2007) "Wittgenstein's Method: Ridding People of Philosophical Prejudices," in G. Kahane, E. Kanterian, and O. Kuusela, eds., *Wittgenstein and His Interpreters*, Oxford: Blackwell, 66–87.

Moyal-Sharrock, D. (2003). "Logic in Action: Wittgenstein's *Logical Pragmatism* and the Impotence of Scepticism," *Philosophical Investigations*, 26(2), 125–48.

Moyal-Sharrock, D. (2004). *Understanding Wittgenstein's On Certainty*, Basingstoke: Macmillan.

Moyal-Sharrock, D. (2015). "Wittgenstein on Forms of Life, Patterns of Life, and Ways of Living," in D. Moyal-Sharrock and P. Donatelli, eds., "Wittgenstein and Forms of Life," special issue, *Nordic Wittgenstein Review*, 21–42.

Moyal-Sharrock, D. (2017). "Fighting Relativism: Wittgenstein and Kuhn," in C. Kanzian, S. Kletzl, J. Mitterer, and K. Neges, eds., *Realism – Relativism – Constructivism*, Berlin: De Gruyter, 215–32.

Müller, J. (1840). "Schlussbemerkungen über die Entwickelungsvariationen der thierischen and menschlichen Lebensformen auf der Erde," in *Handbuch der Physiologie des Menschen für Vorlesungen*, Coblenz: J. Hölscher, 768–78.

Nohl, H. (1938). *Charakter und Schicksal: Eine pädagogische Menschenkunds*, Frankfurt: Verlag Gerhard Schulte-Bulmke.

Nyíri, J. C. (1981). "Wittgenstein's Later Work in Relation to Conservatism," in B. McGuinness and A. Kenny, eds., *Wittgenstein and His Times*, Oxford: Oxford University Press, 44–68.

Padilla Gálvez, J. and Gaffal, M. (2011). "Forms of Life and Language Games. An Introduction," in J. Padilla Gálvez and M. Gaffal, eds., *Forms of Life and Language Games*, Frankfurt: Ontos Verlag.

Pears D. (1995). "Wittgenstein's Naturalism," *The Monist*, 78(4), 411–24.

Pichler, A. and Smith, D. (2013). "A List of Correspondences between Wittgenstein's TS-310 and MS 115ii," in A. Coliva, D. Moyal-Sharrock, and V. A. Munz, eds., *Mind, Language and Action: Papers of the 36th International Wittgenstein Symposium*, Kirchberg am Wechsel: Austrian Wittgenstein Society, 311–18.

Pritchard, D. (2018). "Quasi-Fideism and Religious Conviction", *European Journal for Philosophy of Religion*, 10(3), 51–66.

Putnam, H. (1987). *The Many Faces of Realism*, La Salle, IL: Open Court.

Ritter, J., Gründer, K., and Gabriel, G., eds. (2007). *Historisches Wörterbuch der Philosophie*, Berlin: Directmedia.

Rudder Baker, L. (1984). "On the Very Idea of a Form of Life," *Inquiry*, 27, 277–89.

Russell, B. (1935–6). "The Limits of Empiricism," *Proceedings of the Aristotelian Society, New Series*, 36, 131–50.

Scheman, N. (2017). "Forms of Life: Mapping the Rough Ground," in H. Sluga and D. G. Stern, eds., *The Cambridge Companion to Wittgenstein*, Cambridge: Cambridge University Press, 389–414.

Scheman, N. and O'Connor, P., eds. (2002). *Feminist Interpretations of Ludwig Wittgenstein*, University Park: Penn State University Press.

Schleiermacher, F. (1862). *Psychologie: Aus Schleiermacher's handschriftlichem Nachlasse und nachgeschriebenen Vorlesungen*, Sämmtliche Werke 3, Band 6, ed. L. George, Berlin: G. Reimer.

Schopenhauer, A. (1819). *Die Welt als Wille und Vorstellung*, Munich: Georg Müller.

Schulte, J. (1984). "Chor und Gesetz: Zur 'Morphologischen Methode' bei Goethe und Wittgenstein," *Grazer Philosophische Studien*, 21(1), 1–32.

Schulte, J. (2010). "Does the Devil in Hell Have a Form of Life?," in A. Marques and N. Venturinha, eds., *Wittgenstein on Forms of Life and the Nature of Experience*, Bern: Peter Lang, 125–41.

Schulte, J. (2017). "Surveyability," in H. J. Glock and J. Hyman, *A Companion to Wittgenstein*, Oxford: Blackwell, 278–90.

Schulte, J. (2018). "Wittgenstein's Remarks on Aesthetics and Their Context," in D. G. Stern, ed., *Wittgenstein in the 1930s: Between the Tractatus and the Investigations*, Cambridge: Cambridge University Press, 224–38.

Smith, B. (2017). "Wittgenstein, Naturalism, and Scientism," in J. Beale and I. J. Kidd, eds., *Wittgenstein and Scientism*, London: Routledge.

Snowdon, P. F. (2018). "Wittgenstein and Naturalism," in K. M. Cahill and T. Raleigh, eds., *Wittgenstein and Naturalism*, London: Routledge.

Spengler, O. (1918). *Der Untergang des Abendlandes*, vol. 1, Vienna: Braumüller.

Spengler, O. (1922). *Der Untergang des Abendlandes*, vol. 2, Munich: C. H. Beck.

Spranger, E. (1921). *Lebensformen: Geisteswissenschaftliche Psychologie und Ethik der Persönlichkeit*, 2nd ed., Halle: M. Niemeyer.

Sraffa, P. (1960). *Production of Commodities by Means of Commodities*, Cambridge: Cambridge University Press.

Stern, D. G. (2004). *Wittgenstein's Philosophical Investigations: An Introduction*, Cambridge: Cambridge University Press.

Stroud, B. (1965). "Wittgenstein and Logical Necessity," *The Philosophical Review*, 74(4), 504–18.

Stroud, B. (1984). "The Disappearing 'We': The Allure of Idealism," *Proceedings of the Aristotelian Society, Supplementary Volumes*, 58, 242–58.

Strawson, P. F. (1985). *Skepticism and Naturalism: Some Varieties*, London: Routledge.

Toulmin, S. (1969). "Ludwig Wittgenstein," *Encounter*, 32(1), 58–71.

Turing, A. (1936–7). "On Computable Numbers, with an Application to the *Entscheidungsproblem*," *Proceedings of the London Mathematical Society*, 2(42), 230–65.

Waismann, F. (1965). *The Principles of Linguistic Philosophy*, London: Macmillan.

Williams, B. (1974). "Wittgenstein and Idealism," in G. Vesey, ed., *Understanding Wittgenstein*, London: Macmillan, 76–95.

Winch, P. (1959–60). "Nature and Convention," *Proceedings of the Aristotelian Society, New Series*, 60, 231–52.

Winch, P. (1964). "Understanding a Primitive Society," *American Philosophical Quarterly*, 1(4), 307–24.

Winch, P. (1990 [1958]). *The Idea of a Social Science and Its Relation to Philosophy*, 2nd ed., London: Routledge.

Witherspoon, E. (2003). "Conventions and Forms of Life," in F. F. Schmitt, ed., *Socializing Metaphysics: The Nature of Social Reality*, New York: Rowman & Littlefield, 211–46.

Wittgenstein, L. (1967). *Lectures and Conversations on Aesthetics, Psychology and Religious Belief*, ed. C. Barrett, Berkeley: University of California Press [*LC*].

Wittgenstein, L. (1969 [1958]). *The Blue and Brown Books*, 2nd ed., Oxford: Blackwell [*BBB*].

Wittgenstein, L. (1975 [1969]). *On Certainty*, eds. G. E. M. Anscombe and G. H. von Wright, 2nd ed., Oxford: Blackwell [*OC*].

Wittgenstein, L. (1976). *Lectures on the Foundations of Mathematics: Cambridge 1939*, ed. C. Diamond, Ithaca, NY: Cornell University Press [*LFM*].

Wittgenstein, L. (1978 [1956]). *Remarks on the Foundations of Mathematics*, eds. G. H. von Wright, R. Rhees, and G. E. M. Anscombe, 3rd ed., Oxford: Blackwell [*RFM*].

Wittgenstein, L. (1980). *Remarks on the Philosophy of Psychology*, vol. 1, eds. G. E. M. Anscombe and G. H. von Wright, vol. 2, eds. G. H. von Wright and H. Nyman, Oxford: Blackwell [*RPP I, RPP II*].

Wittgenstein, L. (1981). *Zettel*, eds. G. E. M. Anscombe and G. H. von Wright, 2nd ed., Oxford: Blackwell [*Z*].

Wittgenstein, L. (1982/1992). *Last Writings on the Philosophy of Psychology*, vols. 1 and 2, eds. G. H. von Wright and H. Nyman, Oxford: Blackwell [*LW I, LW II*].

Wittgenstein, L. (1988). *Wittgenstein's Lectures on Philosophical Psychology 1946–47*, ed. P. T. Geach, Chicago: University of Chicago Press [*PGL*].

Wittgenstein, L. (1993). *Philosophical Occasions 1912–1951*, ed. J. Klagge and A. Nordmann, Cambridge: Hackett [*PO*].

Wittgenstein, L. (1998 [1977]). *Culture and Value*, 2nd ed., ed. G. H. von Wright, H. Nyman, A. Pichler, trans. P. Winch, Oxford: Blackwell (1st ed. with English translation [1980], ed. G. H. von Wright, H. Nyman, A. Pichler, trans. P. Winch, Oxford: Blackwell) [*CV*].

Wittgenstein, L. (2000). *Wittgenstein's Nachlass: The Bergen Electronic Edition*, Oxford: Oxford University Press [*BEE*].

Wittgenstein, L. (2001 [1953]). *Philosophische Untersuchungen: Kritisch-genetische Edition*, ed. J. Schulte with H. Nyman, E. von Savigny, and G. H. von Wright, Frankfurt: Suhrkamp [*PU*].

Wittgenstein, L. (2003). *The Voices of Wittgenstein: The Vienna Circle: Ludwig Wittgenstein and Friedrich Waismann*, ed. G. Baker, London: Routledge [*VW*].

Wittgenstein, L. (2005). *The Big Typescript: TS 213*, eds. C. G. Luckhardt and M. A. E. Aue, Oxford: Blackwell [*BT*].

Wittgenstein, L. (2009 [1953]). *Philosophical Investigations*, 4th ed., ed. P. M. S. Hacker and J. Schulte, trans. G. E. M. Anscombe, P. M. S. Hacker and J. Schulte, Oxford: Blackwell (3rd ed. [2001], ed. G. E. M. Anscombe and R. Rhees, trans. G. E. M. Anscombe, Oxford: Blackwell) [*PI, PPF*].

Wittgenstein, L. (2017). *Wittgenstein's Whewell's Court Lectures: Cambridge, 1938–1941*, Oxford: Blackwell [*WCL*].

von Wright, G. H. (1981) "Wittgenstein in Relation to His Times," in B. McGuinness and A. Kenny, eds., *Wittgenstein and His Times*, Oxford: Oxford University Press, 108–20.

von Wright, G. H. (1993). "The Wittgenstein Papers," in L. Wittgenstein, *Philosophical Occasions 1912–1951*, eds. J. Klagge and A. Nordmann, Cambridge: Hackett, 480–510.

Wundt, W. (1908 [1886]). *Ethics: An Investigation of the Facts and Laws of Moral Life*, 2nd ed., London: G. Allen and Unwin, New York: Macmillan.

Acknowledgments

This work would not have been possible without the help and encouragement of many. I want to thank in particular David G. Stern for his constant advice as well as his editorial suggestions; the participants in my graduate seminar on forms of life at University of Califorinia, Irvine (2021), and especially Alice Crary and Juliet Floyd as guests speakers; Almut Kristine von Wedelstaedt for permission to consult her 2007 thesis "Zum Begriff der Lebensform bei Wittgenstein"; Rob Vinten for help in locating some sources; and two anonymous reviewers for their valuable comments. Finally, this work benefited from a Faculty Publication Grant bestowed by the University of California, Irvine Humanities Center.

Cambridge Elements ⹀

The Philosophy of Ludwig Wittgenstein

David G. Stern

University of Iowa

David G. Stern is a Professor of Philosophy and a Collegiate Fellow in the College of Liberal Arts and Sciences at the University of Iowa. His research interests include history of analytic philosophy, philosophy of language, philosophy of mind, and philosophy of science. He is the author of *Wittgenstein's Philosophical Investigations: An Introduction* (Cambridge University Press, 2004) and *Wittgenstein on Mind and Language* (Oxford University Press, 1995), as well as more than 50 journal articles and book chapters. He is the editor of *Wittgenstein in the 1930s. Between the 'Tractatus' and the 'Investigations'* (Cambridge University Press, 2018) and is also a co-editor of the *Cambridge Companion to Wittgenstein* (Cambridge University Press, 2nd ed., 2018), *Wittgenstein: Lectures, Cambridge 1930–1933, from the Notes of G. E. Moore* (Cambridge University Press, 2016) and *Wittgenstein Reads Weininger* (Cambridge University Press, 2004).

About the Series

This series provides concise and structured introductions to all the central topics in the philosophy of Ludwig Wittgenstein. The Elements are written by distinguished senior scholars and bright junior scholars with relevant expertise, producing balanced and comprehensive coverage of the full range of Wittgenstein's thought.

Cambridge Elements ≡

The Philosophy of Ludwig Wittgenstein

Printed in the United States
by Baker & Taylor Publisher Services